# PERMISSION
# TO
# APPROACH?

# Permission to Approach?

The Adventures of an
American Tutor Working
for a Global Family

Jill Mary Kohler

MCP - Maitland, FL

Mill City Press, Inc.
2301 Lucien Way #415
Maitland, FL 32751
407·339·4217
www.millcitypublishing.com

ISBN-13: 978-1-54560-335-2

Printed in the United States of America

*For Michael, 'the keeper,'*
*endless gratitude for all you do…*

# How It All Started...

T he online ad began:
   "Professional couple seeking tutor for our eight-year-old son, Andrew, in Ibiza, Spain. Three-month position..."
   My eyes sped across the type.
   "Creative, experienced, with solid knowledge of American curriculum. Must like hobbit houses, pirate shacks, and elf bungalows, all of which we have on our four-acre Ibizan compound. Position includes private 400 sq. ft. casita, food, and use of car.
   With quivering fingers, I tapped the keyboard and sent the following response to the parents under the guise of writing directly to the student:

Dear Andrew,

Your mom and dad are looking to make you extra smart! They have placed an ad online to find you the perfect tutor. Please show them this note so we can get started on making you the brightest boy in your third-grade class.
   My name is Jill. I'm old but not grandma-old. Well, maybe I *am* grandma old, but check out why I

1

am the perfect teacher. I taught for twenty-nine years…
yepper…in New York. The district nominated me for
New York State Teacher of the Year, and although I
didn't win, just getting the nomination was pretty cool.

Yes, I taught grade four. That is the grade that has
all the standardized tests. Many teachers didn't like
that age, but I did (and still do).

Still certified in NY but now also in Florida, where
I taught and also homeschooled (still do). I planned
on homeschooling for a year, but it's slipped into six!
It's time to pass the baton and see where else I can
be an asset.

My passion is bike riding. Gypsy will be happy to
hear we have a dog as well. He's a rescue and came
with the name Moody. It fits.

Creativity is my middle name. (That's a metaphor,
but I'll teach you that later on.)

When you learn fractions, you get to bake. You also
need to know them so when you grow up your wife
doesn't think you're ill-educated. When you get older,
you'll get that.

So tell me about *you*, Andrew. What do you like to
do? Do you mind your hands getting dirty, and can you
use a hammer? Can you stand on your head or sew on
a button? Do you have friends?

I speak Spanish but not fluently (but pretty well).
Animals are cool, bugs not so much. But kids need

to learn about bugs, so I suck it up and touch them. They look interesting under a microscope...but don't try using a microscope slide with an elephant. They don't fit, and they complain.

So that's about it, Andrew. If the universe wants this connection to continue and God smiles, then we'll write again. This is being penned from a cruise ship. (We cruise monthly (because we're old (well, not *that* old.))

Be safe. Be happy. You're a kid, and that's what kids should do.

Miss Jill (Kohler)
   Later that day, a response from the parents:
   "Hello Jill!

Thank you so much for writing such a thorough and engaging email. It definitely caught our attention, and we got super excited! You sound *great*! Is there a way you would be able to Skype?

We would love for you to "meet" us, and most of all to talk to you more about the position.

The main question would be when you would be available to come. Timing is pretty important for us, as we are planning to leave to Pebble Beach, California, in the middle of July, and for that reason would like to start the "teaching" ASAP.

Hope that you make it happen. Let us know when would work for you to Skype.

Looking forward to talking with you further!"

Ten days later, I landed in Ibiza.

# Who I Am...

To better understand how living with a family of wealth on a Mediterranean island came to be, it's best to understand from where I hail. My roots. A little bit about the unusual folks who made up my family and how a South Florida senior citizen could find herself on an American Airlines flight to a place she's never been. To work for a family without investing in a background check. Crazy? Of course. Would I do it again? In a heartbeat.

Born to an Irish mother and Italian father, my birth was the last hope for a boy. Two sisters preceded me, and at eight and ten years my senior, my debut was somewhat of a surprise. "At least you could have been a boy," my mother reminded me on more than one occasion. Our family surname was retired on my birthday, July 8, 1951.

Born, raised, and educated in New York City, we lived in a two-story row house with a front stoop and back porch. My two sisters shared a bedroom, my grandmother and I shared a twin bed, and my aunt and her daughter slept in the finished basement. We had a single bathroom on the second floor that, of course, my father, the sole male, found impossible to occupy.

We were a happy family with frequent company and Sunday afternoon pasta dinners followed by boisterous card games clouded by a room full of cigarette smoke.

Mom's photo could have been posted in the dictionary next to the word *ostentatious*. When I was a child, she pulled my sled through snowstorms wrapped in her mink coat, stopping to clean the lenses on her rhinestone eyeglasses. Her ruby-red fingernails shared the hue with her lipstick, and while other mothers donned warm hats, my mother didn't want her hair flattened. She loved adventure and slot machines. Not necessarily in that order.

My father was the consummate businessman, generous to a fault. He loved his daughters and delighted in presenting any of us with roses for bringing home an A on our report cards. Straight A's earned you a cake, with your name written in icing, creating competition among us girls.

My sisters married within months of each other. At only ten years old, I was unaware of how the household would change without the girls around. My extended family moved out, and my parents bought a unit on the twelfth floor of a skyscraper. They wintered in Florida and shuffled me between family members who unfortunately had alcohol issues. Stability essentially departed before my eleventh birthday.

High school graduation meant the last of the daughters would be gone, in my case to college, and my parents would be free. They bought me a new car and a set of luggage, sold the house they were living in on Long Island at that point, and purchased a one-bedroom condo in Florida. I was essentially on my own. Maybe it was birth order, maybe just the family's eccentric DNA, but I began to look at life as a playground with infinite opportunities. When I took a semester off in college to spend a month traipsing about Europe, the travel bug adopted my soul.

I earned my bachelor's degree in two and a half years, graduating cum laude, by attending class year-round, as I no longer had a New York residence to go home to. The following year I got my master's degree, a teaching job, and a husband.

Two sons later, I found myself single again. I raised them, put them through college, and traversed life. They have apparently inherited their mother's travel gene and both have journeyed the globe.

Retired to South Florida and subscribed to Match. com. Met a gentleman ten years my senior, Mike, whom I affectionately refer to as "the keeper."

Mike is the antithesis of me. Born in Georgia, he is a conservative, soft-spoken, amour-in-the-dark sort of guy. I hail from New York. A night of passion is lights on, cameras rolling. They say folks from the Big Apple are blunt. I like to say, efficient.

A year after we started dating, we purchased a home in a South Florida senior community. A rescue pup cemented the relationship, and although he has no redeeming qualities (the pup, not Mike), he's part of the family.

# Running it by Friends and Family...

They say there are no coincidences. Sort of believe that. Opportunities meant to happen register with the universe. When your number moves you to the front of the line, you can either accept or dismiss chance.

Sixty-four-year-old grandmother of four, battled the bulge with bike riding; immobilized with thought of flying. Simply driving past an airport triggered anxiety, but now heading to Miami International Airport for an eleven-hour trek to a Spanish island I came to eventually refer to as the Rock.

Answering an online ad sans a background check is why smart women doing stupid things often appear in newspaper headlines. But for some unexplainable reason my "gut" opened the floodgates to what would eventually become infinite adventure.

Ran the idea by Mike expecting some trepidation. He thought it was a colossal opportunity and encouraged me to pursue it. Repeatedly asked if he was OK with this crazy folly, and his response was always the same: "This is an incredible opportunity. You are perfect for the job, and they will be lucky to have you."

Decision made; ironclad agenda secured like gold bars in an armored truck.

Preparing to leave your routine for three months requires a mental blueprint. Visits to the medicine man, related prescriptions, overnights to the children and grandchildren, bills prepaid, and of course a freezer full of meals for "the keeper." A sleepless night before the flight, a prayer for safety and anticipation masked in awe.

The parents of my soon-to-be-student booked the flight. American Airlines. Economy class smack in the middle of a five-across row. Toddler to my right who, on a regular basis, grabbed my armrest, raising the volume on my earphones to shrill mode. The young man on my left apparently boarded the plane after a full day at the gym…without showering. Both seatmates helped make the entire nine-hour first leg…well… memorable.

Repeatedly asked myself how I would have felt if my adult children hopped an airplane to take a job without due diligence. Terms like "sex slave" and "never seen again" whispered caution in my ear. Dismissed doubt with acknowledgment that for a gal my age, or *any* age, this was a tremendous opportunity.

*Dear Diary,*

*Do elder angels shoot opportunities to us or do we create them ourselves? Is taking a job in a foreign country a brainless decision? Am I in a midlife crisis? Would purchasing a red Corvette and becoming a platinum blond have been a safer option to apply salve to my vanishing youth? Did I pack Imodium?*

Sort of an eye-opener to see responses from friends/family when you tell them you're headed to the Mediterranean. To work. For a family you've not met or done a background check on.

I posed the question to a table full of friends, visiting us to celebrate this incredible endeavor: "Do you think they want me for a slave?"

"Seriously? With all the young girls out there, you think they're luring a sixty-four-year-old to Spain?"

"You never know. They saw my photo," I pointed out.

"We think you're safe," they assured me in almost perfect unison.

Dear friends,

Ever feel like you don't have a choice? Happens to me a lot. More than a compelling calling, it's more like an obsession. Opportunities present themselves and it's nearly impossible to say no to the invite.

I leave tomorrow for Spain. Mike and I are off to Walmart. It's the romantic last days to remember. Why aren't we wrapped up in the comforter firing the kiln of heated passion? Rhetorical, don't answer. We're off to Walmart, and not even the lingerie department, either. Sigh...

Each of my sons received instructions if, in fact, their mother was apprehended by masked pirates. Tossed into the hull of a ship. Without sunlight. Or mac and cheese. Or a bike. Notarized the letters and mailed them directly from the post office.

The evening before departure, I sat at the water's edge behind our home. The sun low in the sky, with Moody, my pup, settled in on my lap, his nose twitching to catch myriad scents. We sat about thirty minutes, scrawled the experience in my mind to be retrieved when memories were needed to keep me company in a foreign land.

The enormity of the Madrid-Barajas Airport was daunting. Finding the connecting flight to Ibiza was the impetus for a sweating brow and racing heart. Language barrier and time constraint tested my mettle. Muttered a divine plea, and before long I stood on the boarding line for the one-hour second-segment flight to Ibiza. Did the Miami ticket agents clearly indicate where my three pieces of luggage should be sent? Prayed for same-day arrival. Same airport. Same runway.

# The Arrival...

Tousled hair, puffy eyes, and little transatlantic sleep painted a questionable first impression. The welcoming committee of one was Dad. A strapping 6'3", fifty-eight-year-old Eastern European man with floppy gray curls and captivating eyes. With barely a hint of accent, he threw one arm around me and said, "Thank you for coming, Jill. We really appreciate it. We'll do everything to make this a wonderful experience for you." He maneuvered my luggage through the crowds, directly to the Mercedes SUV conveniently parked nearby. A smile never left his face, and his laughing blue eyes reminded me of Old St. Nick.

Forty-minute drive home. Left the highway, trekked over a small mountain onto an almost-one-lane road, to finally reach the quaint town of San Antonio. Sunbeds, parasols, bars, and attitude combined to flavor the town's success as a destination for European young people.

The dad was quick-witted with a side of sarcasm. Somewhat irreverent, his sense of humor matched mine, and although English was not his native tongue, most times he appropriately responded to punch lines or innuendos. An exception was the idioms stemming from American culture, and a stronger challenge continued in deciphering New York–isms.

*Dear Diary,*

*The dad is adorable. I wonder if he knows my political stance. Would he care? He drives fast, recklessly almost. Should I inquire as to his religious beliefs? He keeps his fingernails trimmed nicely and praises his wife. I wonder if he has digestive issues.*

"I'm looking forward to meeting the rest of the family," I began. "And you have a pup. That's great. I love animals."

"Well, my wife's not home. She'll be out of the country for at least another ten days."

Red flag. Wife not around?

"But she'll be pleased to meet you when she returns."

A pang of uncertainty; fleeting moment of doubt.

The terrain was arid. Moonlike. Orange soil framed by forested mountains. Relatively clean roadways between airport and house. Some spray-painted graffiti reflected artistic tags but no obvious indications of poverty, unemployment, or serious crime.

"What would you like me to call you?"

"Kepler is my formal name. You can call me Kep."

More banal chat until the Mercedes turned sharply at the sea. A single lane, dirt road, etched tire ruts fit the

SUV and with a bouncy ride welcomed us to the four-acre gated compound. Castle-like sliding gate of tall wooden planks. Steel nails, pointed upward, cemented into the top of entranceway deterring unwanted visitors. Unsure at that point which side of the fence I wanted to be on.

Gypsy, a two-year-old mini mixed breed, pranced across the tan-pebbled driveway to welcome us. Her dusty, amber coat concealed bits of scrub, the consequence of infinite through-the-woods ball chasing. At twenty-eight pounds, she looked almost gaunt, the result of a strict dietary regimen. She maneuvered like the cat, who shared both her property and blue frayed bed, and incredibly echoed her with feline-like grace. White, downy fur blanketed the cat who, although feral, had adopted the family several years back. She repeatedly feigned death, encouraging Gypsy to nudge her relentlessly, a game they continuously played. Early evenings the duo would come to share the outdoor lounge chair, whether or not I was on it.

The homestead appeared serene; elegant fields of purple lavender, yellow and pink rose bushes hugging the *piedra del muerto* paths. The special stone was expensive, native to the island and passed down through generations to create formidable walls and walkways. Never painted, its natural beige hue was preferred. No children's chalk drawing permitted. No painted signs. The rocks were admired, almost, revered.

*Dear Diary,*

*I bought all that chalk to do math problems outdoors, and we won't be able to use it. What other restrictions will there be?*

Within minutes, the heavy planked gate slid open once again, revealing a small red car blanketed with orange dust. Young Andrew and Bonita, the house-keeper, smiled through the dirty windshield. Andrew offered a timid wave appropriate for an eight-year-old boy who was meeting his private tutor for the first time.

Kep introduced me to the duo and prefaced the intro-duction with the fact that Bonita spoke no English. Her bright smile and approachable manner welcomed me.

Andrew was eight. Unusually tall, extremely hand-some, and spoke with a strong British accent. His floppy sandy hair rested on his eyelashes. We shook hands and moved into the house for the main meal.

The main meal was a scrumptious ritual. It would become the meeting place for the family and steal at least two hours from each day. Food prepared and served exactly at the same time but not by the same chef. Bonita cooked regularly, but the Wednesday guest chefs were always a surprise. Most were vegetarians, and on more than one occasion, Kep, holding a fork/ knife upright, bellowed, "Where's the meat? I want meat!" After only a week, that same rant included my name: "Jill and I want meat!" His antics were endearing.

*Dear Diary,*

*How sweet Kep is. He's a meat-and-potatoes guy eating under the direction of a vegetarian chef. How did that happen? At what point will he put his foot down and demand meals he actually enjoys? Maybe he is just a "goes along to get along" kind of guy. Then again, he didn't get to where he is by being a wallflower. Is there another side of Kepler? Did he ever mention the word "chained"? Is the wife really out of the country, or is she buried under the elf house? Serial killers sometime seem normal. Gulp.*

Heavy furniture inside the main house. Walls built to keep summer temps at bay, so the homes on Ibiza have twenty-four-inch walls. This particular home had security windows and iron gates that could keep out ill-intentioned folks arriving uninvited. Seating, comfortable white linen chairs, contrasted against the royal blue accessories. Immaculately kept. Understated casual elegance. Vases of live flowers dotted each room strategically placed on dark timber tables. Soft music reverberated through a houseful of hidden speakers.

Tile throughout kept the home comfortably cool. In the small kitchen, ancient slate flooring created a wobbly table. The open stone shelves served to hold dozens of bread and cheese boards often used instead of traditional plates. A tall narrow refrigerator housed mostly produce while eggs and butter sat out at room temperature.

The pantry, about 4'x8', displayed endless rows of naturally jarred and canned products I did not recognize. No prepared foods, no commercial labels. Handwritten identification of each item in shades of brown and black. A tiny window the size of a 33 1/3 record album allowed natural light to filter in. The shadow created thoughts of an old farmhouse where grandmother would store canned summer vegetables.

Our first dinner together, although unfamiliar, was tasty and a tad spicier than I was used to. Fresh vegetables and chicken coated in homemade breadcrumbs were served with French bread and olive oil. Finally, when coffee was served, Andrew was excused from the table. Kep and I continued chatting.

Twenty minutes later Andrew appeared grasping huge plastic balls and rods, connected in random (I thought) configurations.

"Do you want to play DNA, Jill? You go first." The eight-year old offered me the chromosome pieces. A glimpse at his father, hoping he would bail me out, was for naught.

*Dear Diary,*

*Andrew plays DNA? Is that even a game? I'll have to teach him stickball and red light, green light. Was his previous tutor anything like me?*

Main meal completed, it was time to mosey over to my accommodations. The casita, about four hundred square feet, was professionally decorated, loaded with charm, and perfectly functional. Full kitchen, oven/microwave, refrigerator, and more than ample counter space. Rustic table, handmade from pallets and adorned with red place mats and matching seat cushions painted a picture of a storybook cottage. A tall bookshelf constructed of towering driftwood displayed matching red tea sets and vases. Two impressive closets, with glossy yellow doors awaited typical Ibizan attire, not the least bit similar to the retiree's apparel we are used to in South Florida.

The bathroom was large, with several shower adjustments. One could rinse his or her entire body simply by pushing a knob that allowed a full-length flow of water. Another lever did just hair. The lowest was directed to clean feet. High-end plumbing foreshadowed all the other expensive, top-of-the-line items that were evident on the compound.

Outside the casita were manicured gardens, a weathered picnic table, and one beige lounge chair whose cushion repeatedly blew off the seat and, like a pretzel, twisted into odd configurations. The mountain vista was a palette of farms and cliffs, and with constant breezes and an occasional strong gust, the mountain air smelled clean and healthy. Laundry the housekeeper had hung on the line danced horizontally.

Excitement and anticipation as I stood in the casita doorway. My feet were cemented to the threshold and I whispered a prayer of gratitude. Although I felt safe, my chin quivered and my eyes grew moist. I asked myself the question: What am I thinking being in a strange country, on an estate of a family I know nothing about, which by the way, had no physical address. I never actually got an answer to that question.

*Dear Diary,*

*The casita is prettier than I expected. It's immaculate, and they filled the refrigerator with food. There is an unopened bottle of shampoo, other personal supplies, and towels as thick as a pillow-top mattress. Floss and sealed toothbrushes are neatly stacked. Did the father say he was a dentist? Or maybe he just hates bad breath.*

Silence shrouded my new home…until Mr. Rooster introduced himself the following sunrise and every morning thereafter. He was a buddy. Fantasy friend who would never come to know me personally but whose sunrise songs would be the catalyst for my positive attitude and endless gratitude.

For the next three months, nestled under a giant oak, the little casita would be home. Far enough from the main house to create privacy; close enough if there was an emergency.

Dear friends,

Arrived safely. Running on adrenaline. Will try to hit the sack early, but the cool night is just settling in and the views of the Mediterranean are outrageous. This is paradise. No…beyond paradise.

Food left for me in casita refrigerator. Can't read labels. Made tea. Hard water leaves marks on counters and glasses. Wondering what hard water does to hair. Curly, gray hair. Maybe it dyes it black, makes it grow, and reduces thigh circumference. Maybe not.

Slept ten hours last night. Finally body and wall clock in synch.

Piano available. Breaks the silence of the compound. Pool is stunning but too cold to swim in yet. Miss Mike.

First full day on compound as the unpacking began in earnest, I realized the electrical cord for my laptop was missing in action. There were several other cords packed, but of course those wouldn't charge the HP.

Hesitated in asking Kepler to take me to town, to the only electrical store within thirty miles of the house.

"No problem. Meet me at the car; I'll run in and get my keys," he cheerfully offered.

He parked the SUV on the street, and with laptop in carrying case, we walked up to the glass counter at the back of an enormous electronics shop. Kep leaned over, resting his chin on his hands. I mimicked him as the patient clerk unwrapped no less than six cords, hoping one would fit. I reached inside the computer bag and found a secret zippered section. I pulled out the missing cord, and noticed it said HP on a small white label.

"Kep. Oh my God. I just found the cord after this woman opened all those sealed packages. Who's going to tell her we found it?" Our heads were less than a foot apart, hunched over the counter.

"Not me," he whispered. "I have an idea. You slip out to the car. I'll look around the store and then just leave." And like two naughty children, that's exactly what we did. We giggled on the way home, and the fact that he could laugh so easily was endearing.

To break the ice and satisfy their need to entertain me, Kep and Andrew took me on walks.

"Is this about how much you walk in Florida?"

"No, I walk to the mailbox and back."

Silence.

Dear friends,

No regrets. The best. No, *better* than the best. Never privy to how special life could be...beats crocheting in the recliner of South Florida.

Dad is a delight and has taken me on *short* fifty-minute walks. Wants me to let him know when I'm ready for the *long* walks.

*Dear Diary,*

*I promise to lay off the Oreos.*

# Irina

## The Lady of the House...

B orn in the United States, Andrew was a late-in-
life baby to an Eastern European mother who,
previously married, had two adult daughters. She was
a grandmother in name only, as her fifty years on the
planet duped the average person into believing she was
ten years younger. A hint of Botox and an inordinate
amount of aerobics, accompanied by vegetarian food,
kept Irina in size 1 clothing. Long brown hair and min-
imal makeup complemented a large smile and obvious
accent. Earlier in her life she was a concert pianist.
European venues as well as New York's Carnegie Hall
reverberated with her Steinway performances. The
middle child, Irina had a much older sister as well as
a younger sister a full generation behind her. Painting
lessons, dance instruction, and a short stint at a Swiss
boarding school created a well-rounded woman whose
strongest virtue was determination. She and Kep made
a striking couple. Almost an appearance of royalty but
without pretense, they were the perfect host/hostess to
their new American tutor.

"Jill, we have a fully equipped gym, if you'd like to use it. We also hike and swim laps."

I figured this was not a good time to mention the stash of potato chips I'd brought along.

"Thank you for the info. I'll try to get into the gym," I muttered meekly.

Irina checked her watch. "Let's say in two hours we meet there."

Didn't realize it then, but that was the beginning of "suggestions" that would continually morph into directives.

*Dear Diary,*

*Seriously? Can't believe there's a gym here. And it's used regularly! Are my hidden Malomars contraband?*
*Physically and mentally exhausted.*

Dear friends,

Milk is not refrigerated. Oranges go in the juicer each morning. Now understand what the Mediterranean diet is. No processed food. Student asks for apple or banana for a snack. Introduced him to Cracker Jacks I brought over. Oh boy.

# The Ibizan Compound

## Home Sweet Temporary Home...

The four-acre compound sported an elf cabin, hobbit house, and other professionally constructed designs any child would cherish. But if one didn't have friends with whom to play, the structures were meaningless. No local children, the family invited a friend over each Saturday to climb, swing, and ultimately endure a multi-hour game of Monopoly. When the weather warmed, the enormous saltwater pool kept everyone occupied.

Dear friends,

Play is an important part of a child's life. But *play* here is full-throttle. Want a pirate ship? With pirate clothes and a dungeon? Metal doors that would keep out a missile? Did I mention a full-size hobbit house? With thatched roof?

First caveat of new job: Dad gave me a phone I'm to answer every time. Didn't recognize the ring and didn't know how to use it anyway. Directed to keep it on me at all times. Finally asked Dad how to answer the darn phone. He replied it was the same button that puts on the delicate cycle in the laundry room. Apparently he has an edgy sense of humor.

Went to town with neighbors. Four of us ordered pizza and two had beers. Bill was seventy euros, about seventy-five dollars. Say what?

Hard water. Bad hair. Period. Drinking water is bottled, but showering? Nope.

Do I still love this decision? Absolutely.

Ibiza has little rain, which accounts for the moon-like appearance shrouded in tangerine soil. Cars, bikes, and pets were dusted with orange, and trying to keep them clean was in vain. When windshield visibility was impossible, the driver poured bottled water on the glass. One wiper swish and you were ready to go. Sometimes the license plate was so encrusted with the rusted hue it could not be read. No one cared, least of all the police.

Policia in Ibiza adhered to subjective enforcement. Sometimes an infraction was punished, other times, ignored. For that reason, the police force scared me. Reminded me of the old boys' club, and I tried to avoid eye contact and stayed within the speed limit, maneuvering along the narrow roadways.

# Nose to the Grindstone...

Even with maximum jet lag, I was anxious to start "work." Called my student into the casita to get to know him. Five minutes into the introductory meet and greet, it was obvious this little boy was extraordinary. Bright. Witty. British accent that he would eventually lose to a New York tutor. Animated, Andrew used exaggerated facial expressions and flailing arm movements to make a point. Literally, every class was a joy. Well, almost every one.

"Jill, I'm just not into this today," he told me one afternoon.

"Oh, really? Why is that?"

"Issues," he said matter-of-factly.

"What sort of issues does an eight-year-old have?"

"Do you know the show *Shark Tank*? It's all about negotiating."

"Yes. Is that an issue for you?"

"Well, I negotiated with somebody at school. My *best* soccer card. He was going to trade me ten not-so-good cards for my *really* good one. But he stole mine and didn't give me *any* of his."

I paused for a moment to capture his full attention.

"Let me tell you about the streets of New York. When I was your age..." I began. "...and the other kid got a black eye even before I was finished with her," I concluded.

And that's how my charge and I became best buds.

*Dear Diary,*

*I love this little boy. Andrew reminds me of my own sons when they were young. He seems kind and sensitive. Fifty states from which to hire a tutor, and his parents chose a native New Yorker.*

*Note to self: you're not in New York. Soften your soul.*

Dear friends,

Seriously don't deserve this bit of heaven. Sitting on picnic bench outside casita. Gypsy, an adorable mixed variety canine that the family adopted, and their outdoor cat are busy playing. It's 11:45 in the morning and total silence on this mountaintop. Took Gypsy for a leashless walk to the sea. Solitude except for a little lost truck whose driver asked for directions in Spanish.

Slipped into a new pair of capris I picked up right before leaving Florida. Now need a belt to keep them up. No junk food. Only food I can't pronounce and probably wouldn't want to know from where it originates.

Casita is full of fruit housekeeper buys for me. Would donate a kidney for a piece of chocolate. Both kidneys if it had almonds.

# A Slice of Princess...

Irina lived a "day camp" life. After Bonita prepared breakfast, the aerobic coach pulled through the gate. Two hours later, the yoga teacher arrived. A shower and outfit change and Irina headed to greet the tennis instructor she met three times weekly. Back in time for main meal and out again for waxing, manicure, or hair salon.

*Dear Diary,*

*I want Irina's life. Maybe I'd volunteer or do something productive, though. She is so gracious. Is it genuine?*

One evening Andrew was a messenger. "Jill," he began, "my mom wants you at the house for champagne."

That was probably a defining moment. Sweet tea in the Sunshine State and champagne on a Mediterranean island are galaxies apart.

*Dear Diary,*

*The last time I had champagne was on New Year's Eve. In 1986.*

*Note to self: champagne contains alcohol. Broomsticks are not dance partners. Send text with apologies.*

# Time on Their Hands...

Irina traveled to mainland Europe for shopping and medical care. Their Croatian residence, eleven rooms in a historic apartment building, allowed her to commute without luggage. The three-day scheduled jaunts generally turned into ten. Sometimes a stopover in another country to visit family left Andrew home alone with Kep. Bonita cooked, cleaned, and did their laundry. And as the tutor, the benefits dribbled over to the casita.

Weekends were playtime. Not only for Andrew but for the family, extended family, or anyone lucky enough to be on the compound. Exclusive restaurants tucked into mountainsides with breathtaking vistas or yacht rentals could be on the agenda.

Part of wealth is the ability to enjoy spontaneity. Hopping a flight to Venice or Barcelona, Munich or Krakow was commonplace.

"How cool that you can get away any time you want," I said. "Not even sure where I'd choose if I could simply blink and head for any global city." I thought for a moment. "The Oktoberfest in Munich. That's where I'd choose. How fun would *that* be?" I offered to no one in particular.

"Then that is where we shall go," chimed in Kep. "You and me. We will fly to Munich through Madrid. I have a business meeting I must attend first. You will go directly to the hotel, and I will meet you there in the evening. Do not eat dinner. There is a special place I want to take you."

That night, I lay awake staring at the planked casita ceiling. This job is a fairy tale, I thought.

*Dear Diary,*

*Seriously?*

Dear friends,

Having mornings off is seventeen steps higher than spectacular. Four walled acres on a cliff with the sole sound of a faraway rooster is the epitome of heaven. Haven't made any friends yet, and loving this so much, not really in the mood to meet anyone.

Strolled through a town called San Carlos. Found a *farmacia* and bought a small bottle of nail polish remover. For a 59-cent bottle, I paid 3.60 euros. Figured it came to five bucks for that little container. Lucky that food is supplied on this job. *Very* lucky.

Taught two hours. Neighbor invited student and me to Mexican restaurant. Establishment opens at 8:30 pm.

I begged off to hit the sack, but student joined them. Slept nine hours and fifty minutes.

Everything is later here. Get up each morning between eight and ten a.m.

Laundry room is a wing that you enter from the outside of the house. Near the casita, but...there are many machines in there and can't figure out the deal. Grabbed the housekeeper for her to explain which I should use. She spoke *no* English. Brain fried before I got my morning tea, but managed to push enough buttons to get clothes washed. Everything gets hung outside and is dry in an hour.

The compound has its own weather pattern. Still or soft breeze in daylight, but when darkness falls, hold on to your hat. Howls like a hurricane. Seriously, every night.

# Remembering You Are the "Help"...

When you're hired, you have a boss. You're the employee, or in this case, the "help." Treated like family most times, there are events that reconfirm you are at work.

Fresh out of the pool, hanging laundry on the outdoor line, Kep stopped by.

"We are going to Taco Paco. Please be ready in twenty minutes."

"If you don't mind, I'll pass. My hair is full of saltwater and I want to get these clothes hung."

"Then meet us at the gate in *thirty* minutes."

Not an option, just a compromise of time.

Another time, Irina strolled by the casita. "Jill, we are heading to Café del Mar. Can you be ready in five minutes?"

"Irina, I really appreciate you always inviting me along. But this time I'm tired and would love to lounge and read my book." In a graceful spin, she disappeared, and while she moved like a princess, she had the determination of a lightweight boxer.

A roaring voice accompanied stomping footsteps on the pebbled casita walkway. "Jill. What is this I hear you are not joining us at Café del Mar? Do you not know what that is?" asked Kep.

"I just want to hang on the compound. Me and Gypsy, the tennis ball, and crazy cat. We'll keep an eye on the place. You go enjoy a nice romantic date with Irina. You can leave Andrew here and ignite some romance," I added with a wink.

"*No*. We want you there. Please be ready quickly. We have reservations. *I really want you to see this place.*"

And that became the code phrase for "nonnegotiable." When those words were uttered, you could expect the invite to be extraordinary.

Since Ibiza is mountainous, elegant restaurants as well as local eateries were often perched on cliffs. Overlooking the vertical drop where no railings or walls were constructed were hundred-foot descents generally ending at the sea. Endless vistas of azure ripples were framed by copper soil. Herculean boulders jutted out of the Mediterranean in an imaginary display of brawn. It was impossible to guess their size in the distance. An occasional cruise ship sailed by like a ghostly shadow enveloped in misty fog.

# The Eats...

European food differs greatly from what we Americans consume. Menus of vegetable dishes and fish, served whole, including the head, are commonplace. Seafood, particularly squid, is a staple before a main course, sometimes breaded and disguised, other times not. With heartier appetites, the Europeans eat every part of the catch, never doubting the edible quality of eating fish eyes and the like. Compared to our counterparts across the pond, we Americans are really picky eaters. Then how did we get so fat?

First time main meal had fish on the menu, laughter overtook the table's silence. Tried in vain to regain composure, but an entire fish occupying most of the plate's real estate was comical. He lay on his side with wide-opened eyes and created an invisible icebreaker with which to start a conversation.

"Well now, Mr. Pesce. You probably didn't know you'd be on a blue platter today, did you? Not a good choice, grabbing hold of that bait." I picked up my fork. "Your wife probably sent you out for a quart of milk, and look where you ended up. Now where to start?"

Kep leaned over the table and grabbed my plate. In twenty-eight seconds he deboned the critter and returned to me a clean filet. Eternally grateful, I looked around at the others. Everyone knew exactly how to ready their seafood. Even Andrew. And no one considered an entire fish resting across their plate even remotely humorous.

Couldn't help myself. Opened the fish's mouth and inserted a French fry. Bit my lip to refrain from confirming Americans are crude. Especially if you hail from New York.

We Americans have a relationship with fish. We win them in carnivals. We purchase them and have expensive tanks displayed in our vestibules. But in Europe, it's a war. The winner fillets the loser.

After all this time, this old gal still prefers Twinkies and pastrami on rye (not together).

*Dear Diary,*

*Download the book* Culinary Sophistication. *Read it. Twice. And do two Hail Marys for being immature. Add three Our Fathers for being a jerk. Amen.*

Dear friends,

Taught today. Lunched at main meal, which I initially thought would be boring. It is anything but. Having a big meal prepared for you is too cool. Wish I had a housekeeper.

Hung more laundry on the triple parallel lines under an overcast sky. Hummed and sang songs while pinning each garment. Sometimes I want to cry...I'm just so happy here.

Dad flew in from a quick jaunt over to mainland Europe. Brought me three eleven-dollar bars of pure chocolate. I returned two to the fridge at the main house.

These thighs are looking like bologna logs.

Dad is a specialist in riot statistics plus being an MD. He's a numbers guy whose research indicates that riots are mostly comprised of males between twenty and twenty-three years of age. Since the Syrians entered Europe, those numbers have exploded, and with all the other stats, he truly believes a six-month *no services* meltdown will be soon to occur.

Texting and emailing but missing the voice of Mike and all of you. Miss my family. Homesick? No way. Would I love to beep myself to South Florida for a day and come back here? Of course!

Invited to an exclusive restaurant. *Very* exclusive. Check was just under five hundred dollars for four of us. A fish the size of Seattle was presented on an enormous tray. The head and tail visible, the rest smothered under a mound of white sea salt. Blood pressure spiked just looking at it. But...as usual, it was fantastic.

Salad with goat cheese and cruise-like potato ensemble. Using the bathroom ploy, I slipped away from the table to pick up the check. The family was not happy when they discovered what I had done.

# Maybe I *Do* Need a Friend...

While Andrew attended the little village school, my time was my own. But loneliness set in, and despite Irina and Kepler attempting to include me in their lives, I needed to reach out on my own. An ad on Ibiza Residents, an offshoot of Facebook, introduced me to a delightful British couple now residing on the island.

"Hi there," wrote Grant. "We will be dancing at Cala Pada this Sunday at 3 p.m. Look for us. We'd love to meet you and show you around." They signed their names.

Cala Pada was a beach. With music. And tons of Brits and Germans my age, with no pretenses. For five euros, about $6.50, you could buy a pitcher of sangria. With tons of fruit and just the right amount of "kick" to get you up and boogying in the sand. No partner needed. Sunglasses and rhythm, a smile, and the right attitude could take you into the evening.

Cala Pada became a Sunday staple.

Judith, late sixties, blond, with happiness in her heart, took the proper British role. Her husband, donning a Bahama hat and colorful shirts, had a bit of the devil in him. Irreverent, he had me laughing uncontrollably every time we met. They've been married for half a century and still genuinely refer to each other as "darling."

Contacted them during the draft of this book.

"Do you want me to use your real names or would you like to give me a name to use?"

From Grant: "Describe me as devastatingly handsome with long locks of hair." He continued, "And spell my bloody name right!"

Grant truly was handsome. A confirmation, however, that bald is beautiful.

Several mornings Judith would ring me to meet in Santa Eulalia, the much larger town in which they lived. With no vehicle of their own, they could easily manage life walking to shops and entertainment. We'd meet on the sea and sip glasses, rather than traditional cups, of coffee.

Irina suggested I invite the Brits over to the compound. Did so, but as was not unusual, the lady of the house left the country. Kepler was not thrilled that "the help" was having company, but he made himself scarce and allowed us to use the pool and enjoy sangria at the casita before we all left the compound for dinner. Had Irina been around, she would have prepared hors d'oeuvres, turned on the sound system, and joined in the visit. It was just a difference in personalities.

*Dear Diary,*

*So glad I met the Brits. They are fun and are constantly smiling. They dance on the beach like newlyweds. Could they actually be that happy, or are they funneling poppy seeds off their bagels?*

# In Nomine Patris et Filii et Spiritus Sancti...

## (In the Name of the Father and the Son and the Holy Spirit)

Another attempt at assimilating into Ibizan life took me to the Catholic church where on certain Sundays the Mass was in English. Slipped into a skirt and headed the eight miles to find the building. Sandwiched between storefronts, I never imagined the church would be so grand. About half full, everyone spoke English. They introduced themselves to me and offered to show me the island.

Mass lasted more than an hour. Not because of dramatic Epistles or priestly lectures but because the music director insisted on playing the same hymn four times in a row. The whole song. One, two, three, *four* times. My ADHD hit overdrive and I began counting the number of people wearing glasses. Then narrowing down to reading or full-time glasses. Then the color of the eyewear. At that point, it was obvious, this church was visited for the last time.

When you live in a new locale, it's almost a game to integrate into the culture. The challenge was the language, not Spanish but the island's own: Catalan. It's different enough to cause problems.

*Dear Diary,*

*I wonder if the church music director gets paid by the minute?*

Dear friends,

Every day is a learning experience, and if you are not the type to go with the flow, teaching in Europe is not for you.

Living on a rock, literally. Everything is expensive. Half filled the VW to the tune of 30 euros. It cost 2.17 euros a *liter*, and there are about four liters in one gallon. Do the math.

Dad insisted I join him at a local birthday party. No one spoke English, but I was fine trying my hand at what Spanish I remembered from high school. Pulled up a white plastic chair and integrated into a table full of Spanish "old guys." They welcomed me and turned out to be fun.

Pig and lamb cooking. Heads still attached. Enormous black dog ambled about partygoers with GoPro camera attached to his back. Four hours later Dad asked me to join him and his son to pick up Andrew's friend from the other side of the island. Nice opportunity to see more of the Rock. Back to compound where I headed to casita.

"Jill, please come to the main house. We are setting up the game." I inquired as to *what* game. "Monopoly," he replied. I tried to beg off. "We play every Saturday night, and we'd like you to join us." Hail Mary, full of grace…

# A Hippie Market...

I biza is where old hippies go to die. They bail society and live like they did in the 1960s, with dreadlocks and granny dresses. Some go barefoot while others don homemade sandals. They smoke pot and dabble on their guitar in hope of collecting funds to support their alternative lifestyle.

A few times each week, acres of an empty lot were filled with folks peddling their wares. Some of the creative crafts command a hefty sum while other pieces cost only a few euros. Selling enough of even the less expensive items brought in plenty of tax-free income.

Hippies have their own "constitution." Raising children, and what clothes to wear in public, were up for interpretation. On one bizarre occasion, a man was strolling through the hippie market with a woman attached to him by a dog collar. Absolutely naked (the woman, not him). No one threw them out, and many never flinched an eyebrow. It was Ibiza, and it was the life of hippies.

"Jill, we're headed to the hippie market. This particular one has live music and we can grab a beer and hot dog," announced Kep one afternoon.

Two other family members who happened to be visiting the compound joined us. We stayed about an hour and a half, tapping our toes to the intoxicating beat and singing along to the few songs we recognized.

Dear friends,

Spent time at the hippie market. Throwback from college days. Family left for dinner and I slipped into nightgown to make some calls to the States. Love being on the compound alone. The feral cat climbed on my shoulders to deposit fleas or other Ibizan vermin while I digested the mountain vistas from the lounge chair. Silence. Magical. Rearranged casita furniture and did lesson plans. Not homesick.

*Dear Diary,*

*When you stick your toe into the swimming pool of life, you can envision it being the portal to one of two options: existing or living; treading through to the march of mundane music, or being an elixir of zest. Like double caffeine. How many of us allow our big toe to determine whether or not we take the plunge? If we say it's cold, we're out. The recliner becomes our home and the newspaper our comforter. I took the plunge. Blinded by a dream, fertilized by my significant other, who encouraged me and assured me my student would greatly benefit.*

# Gigs We Never Knew About...

International tutoring is more popular than you would think. Families of wealth who enjoy residences on multiple continents require education options because of frequent travel. Traditional school can be inconvenient or even impossible for families whose jobs require frequent transition. They pay salaries based on experience; some I've seen advertised as high as $150,000 a year. Included in the position are private accommodations, food, and endless opportunities to join in country clubs, galas, and flying or yachting trips about the globe. The perks often outweigh the salary.

Since tutoring and homeschooling are distinctly different, the number of hours worked varies tremendously. A homeschool teacher is expected to cover all the subjects and instructs based on either British or American standards. Very often, the student will be expected to pass rigorous admissions tests for prestigious boarding schools or universities, and it is the job of the tutor to insure admission.

Teaching and living on global yachts offers opportunities for the student to experience firsthand what is being taught. Each port becomes a textbook, and an outstanding educator will incorporate geographical or historical sites into the lesson. The parents will assign a driver to escort the teacher and his/her charge. Because most of us are not privy to this type of enormous resource, we tend to be concerned with value. In this realm, cost is irrelevant. Initially a challenge to overcome, within six months it becomes second nature to the tutor.

When you are employed by families of wealth, there are parameters you are expected to meet. Proper behavior, appropriate appearance, calm demeanor, and perfect etiquette are the minimum. Knowledge of royal protocol is often a prerequisite. No whining, personal demands, or drama accepted. A five-syllable noun is paramount: *flexibility*.

If you are uncomfortable changing residences on a moment's notice, getting packed and ready for the driver to scoop you to the airstrip, this type of work would not be a good fit. When your employer wants to leave the city, country, or continent, you have to be cheerfully prepared to join him.

There are many websites that hire tutors. Their names may suggest that they deal exclusively in nannies, but poking around often brings you to the education component. On these sites are often positions for personal assistants. You can also find schools that teach proper etiquette and certify you to work with international children.

Craigslist could also be an option, found under the heading *education*. Sometimes the placement calls for temporary help. That would generally mean you travel with the family during vacations or holidays.

Several ads caught my eye. One was on a "fully staffed" compound teaching one ten-year-old. The published offering continued: "must be comfortable with armed security and large guard dogs." It was in Moscow. Russia in January?

Monaco had several opportunities posted. One particularly intrigued me, and if I was twenty years younger, I would have applied without hesitation. In bold type: "Must be comfortable with helicopter transport between yacht and dock." Surely this is a world more retired teachers could be investigating.

Sometimes you need to go through "the back door." If you're serious about pursuing global positions, be prepared to do your homework. Some are for American families as well but generally entail visits to their European residences at some point.

The opportunities exist, and the families seeking teachers want experienced educators. Senior teachers are a hot commodity as long as you can physically keep up with the demands of the job.

*Dear Diary,*

*Why aren't I twenty years younger?*

Dear friends,

How am I faring? Fall into bed at night. Lost weight eating things with no labels. If it grows, they eat it. If it's manufactured, good luck finding it.

School function today. Mom is abroad, so I attended with Dad and student. Meat and more meat on jury-rigged grills. Dad insisted I try some and wouldn't let me pay. "They do not take money from Americans," he told me. "Since the War."

Back to compound, where I managed to grab a minute on the casita lounge chair. Gypsy asleep on my lap, interfering with my attempt at crocheting, but I didn't mind. First time I'd had private time.

Dad sauntered down and picked up a broken animal skull off the pebbles under my lounge. "You done with this?"

"No, I'm still working on it," I replied. And that's how the repartee began.

Matches are required to light the casita stove.

"Would you mind bringing another box of matches when you think of it?" I asked.

"What? I counted ninety sticks. That should bring you to July 15. Do you need lessons on lighting the stove?" More wit. The man is entertaining.

In a serious moment, Kep sought reassurance that the tutor is content.

"Jill, are you happy here? Is there anything we can get for you?"

"Well, let me think. I'm on the top of a mountain. I work two hours daily and have free room, board, and a car. The man of the house has special coffee he's handing me with frothy milk. Hmmm...let me see if I'm happy."

# The Road to Wealth...

How do families accumulate such wealth? Hard work, brilliant ideas, or inheritance. Kepler hailed from comfortable surroundings but made his fortune through medical inventions. Patents and royalties are benefits of having an MD under your belt, and with an IQ in the genius range, carrying an idea to fruition obviously brings extraordinary rewards. Like at least six residences, fully staffed on multiple continents. With a personality removed of any pretense, you would never guess this man was so accomplished. While he speaks several languages, heads a myriad of companies, I'm told he still leaves his socks on the floor. He loves *Shark Tank* and despises vitamin supplements. He teased me unmercifully about my pharmacy of Omega meds, cinnamon tablets, and turmeric capsules.

Kep is the oldest of three children, his twin sisters just thirteen months younger than he. Raised as atheist, both sisters, after an apparent epiphany, shocked the family by joining a convent in Northern France. He rarely mentions them. Incredibly, his parents are still living, but speak little English and have settled in Heidelberg, Germany.

Approaching fifty and never married, Kepler met Irina on a dating website. They courted and married a year later.

A Bavarian palace, horse-drawn coaches, and full orchestra completed their fairy-tale wedding. Kep took me there on one of the many "field trips" he organized. Approachable only by boat, the island's palace housed the two hundred wedding attendees. Kep's tux and Irina's handmade lace gown painted a picture of royalty.

A magazine with national recognition featured the couple on its cover. Irina had it framed and it is presently adorning a hallway in their Spanish home.

*Dear Diary,*

*How do you meet a prince on a dating website? When I met Mike, I recall saying, "Seeking my prince." A radio announcer rang my doorbell instead...and we're happy even if we only own one residence and an unruly rescue pup.*

# Getting to Know the Boss...

On a regular basis, Kepler moseyed over to the casita just to visit or discuss Andrew's lesson. Sometimes, however, I think he was just bored when his wife was AWOL.

"Jill, permission to approach?"

"When are you going to stop asking if you can approach? You own the darn place. You can come over whenever you want."

"Well, you might not be decent."

"I'm decent. You hired me, didn't you?"

"Yeah, without a background check. I didn't know your ancestors spoke Albanian."

"What are you talking about? Mom was Irish. Dad Italian. Where's the Albanian coming from?

"Did your ancestry based on your maiden name. Spent hours locating information on Tartrano."

"Well, that was a waste. My maiden name was Tratona."

He laughed heartily at the fact that he had made a mistake, but still found humor in his foible. That admirable trait spoke volumes. He continued: "Let's go for a ride. I'll show you the island and we can stop for coffee."

Wherever we stopped would surely be charming, with sunshine breezes tanning our faces and rustling our curls.

It's funny; there are some folks you connect with immediately. Kep's sense of humor literally kept me in the mood of constant mirth. Dry wit fueled by extraordinary intelligence. Very special employer/employee repartee.

*Dear Diary,*

*This island is spectacular. Having a resident tour guide is a major benefit, especially one who can laugh at his own foibles. Journeying up the side of a mountain in a four-wheel-drive with a very aggressive driver is dicey. At least he's a doctor. If we crash, he can treat me. Unless, of course, he's dead.*

*Note to self: Find out if my life insurance policy is paid up.*

Early one evening, double footsteps shuffled on pebbled walkway. "Jill, permission to approach?" Andrew and his dad looked like lost souls. "We were wondering if you wanted to stroll the promenade in Santa Eulalia and maybe get an ice cream." To a family so weight-conscious, an ice cream was a significant treat.

"I'd love to!" We piled into the SUV, through the gate, and into town.

Evenings on the Mediterranean were spectacular. Mosaic tiles paved the walkways accommodating Europeans strolling arm in arm. No one in a hurry, old and young alike, shuffling down the endless promenade. Outdoor cafés lined the walk, sounds of music wafting from each venue.

Andrew ran ahead, and in keeping with European tradition, Kep offered me his arm. We strolled along the route blending in with the hundreds of souls blessed to live on this fabulous island.

*Dear Diary,*

*This field trip was sane, normal. No scary mountain roads. Ice cream was to die for. Wish I could get Mike here to see the moored sailboats and the shore of the sea. This is paradise, and I hope it never ends.*

"Jill, I am going to the airport. My wife remembered where she lived! I will be back shortly," Kep said the following day.

For the first time, I noticed my employer as a regular man, eager to greet his wife after being apart. He adored Irina and for reasons unknown called her Tink. Probably short for Tinkerbell, which was ironic because neither was American.

Unlike Kep's deliberate footsteps, Irina sashayed like a ballerina…graceful and delicate. She didn't think his humor was much more than immaturity. A slight air of arrogance sifted out now and then, but not nearly enough for me not to like her. She had a good heart, and while her own needs came first, her purpose was to be sure everyone around her was happy as well. To meet that goal, more than extravagant spending was necessary. Not that the folks on the receiving end minded a more sedate engagement or outing, but Irina felt the need to overdo, overspend, over-impress. Kep tried in vain to curb his wife's spending but after a while realized it was a futile task. He once relayed the European version of "You can't take it with you." He would start out with a furrowed brow and then, with an exaggerated shoulder shrug, say, "It's just money, and you can't eat it."

# Ibiza, the Island...

Ibiza is 220 square miles and belongs to the Balearic Islands, a part of Spain. In winter, about 150,000 people live there, but in summer the population explodes. Every hotel is occupied, and it's not uncommon to see posts on trees or social media begging for a bed/couch to rent. Mostly young, fit Europeans find their way to the "party island," where famous discos, such as Pasha, open their doors at midnight. Up to twelve thousand revelers party under one roof dancing to electronic music often next to the likes of Paris Hilton and other American celebrities. I once asked what you wear to the famous discos. "As little as possible," was the response.

Ibiza has a flavor. Distinctive. Flowy, fringe, dreamcatcher sort of feeling. Wreaths of local flora encircle the heads of hippie-like women, whose hair drapes well down their backs. Rows of bracelets climb their arms, and multiple rings adorn each finger. Underwear is optional, and most choose to go commando. Crepe blouses are transparent and bras are essentially nonexistent.

Body waxing is expected. Men's chests and underarms are bare, and I'm told "manscaping" is the norm.

Eyebrows and legs are waxed and the salons market themselves as unisex.

The official languages are Spanish and Catalan, and schoolchildren are taught both. The abundant German population as well as the British contingency makes for a truly global destination.

*Dear Diary,*

*My khaki capris don't fit in here. Will hit town to purchase new duds. I wonder if I'll ever adopt the Ibizan lifestyle. They live life with vitality and no guidelines. How does it feel to go without underwear?*

*Note to self: women whose upper anatomy is described using the letter* D *cannot go braless.*

Naively attempted to purchase a pair of shorts in town. The woman looked at me like a scanner, from head to toe:

"We do not have clothes your size. I am sorry."

I wear a 14, not tremendous by US standards. All their clothing could be described as leggings, in size small, generally worn with a flimsy tunic. And lots of necklaces, long, dangling earrings, and leather flip-flops. Funky. Hippie. Flower children. With no fat and straight teeth.

*Dear Diary,*

*Lay off the sweets.*

Purchasing produce requires a mortgage payment, except for Valencia oranges, which are grown a ferry ride away. Residents of Ibiza easily pick their own lemons and limes from trees that despite little rain grow beautifully on the island.

It's an "anything goes" slice of paradise, where bathing nude is never the exception. Marijuana is smoked in public, and the laissez-faire ambience percolates through generations.

Stores close from one p.m. to four p.m. but reopen and are active until at least ten o'clock at night.

Long hair, bronze tans, and lithe bodies populate Ibiza. An overweight senior from South Florida stands out like a porcupine in a box of puppies.

Dear friends,

Dropped the designer shades, threw open the door, and shut off the heater. It's *Good morning, Ibiza*! Fifty-five sun-rising degrees. A new day for the rooster and I to thank the Lord for spectacular beauty.

Slept nine hours. Can't say living healthy is a bad thing, for sure.

Overcast day. Housekeeper was out sick, and while there were workers all about, their job had nothing to do with putting the main meal on the old galleon table at 2:15. Dad took student and me out for Chinese lunch. Nothing like our Chinese food. Nothing. First of all, the Chinese woman greeted us with "Buenos Dias," which for some reason hit my funny bone. Restaurant was gorgeous, immaculately clean, and the Chow Mein was anything but. More of a spaghetti covered with beef. Never tap water; they ask if you want sparkling or flat. Bill for the three of us came to fifty-four euros, or about fifty-nine dollars.

Breakfast this morning was little yogurt cups, cherry tomatoes, and sunflower seeds. A pear followed, then two cups of green tea. The weight is falling off, but unfortunately the wrinkles arrived from the loss. I look five years older than when I stepped foot on this continent.

# Let's Make a Deal...

Andrew's negotiating skills parallel those of an adult. Every lesson, suggestion, and options for learning were negotiated.

"Let's start with math today," I'd suggest.

"You know, Jill, if we start with playtime, I'll be in a better mood to learn," he replied. "Don't you want me to be cooperative during the lesson?"

"If we don't begin with math, I won't be happy. Don't you want *me* to be cooperative during the lesson?" I paused for effect. "Did you ever see an old lady who is not happy? Not pretty, my little man. Not pretty at all. Now, would you like to begin with fractions or number lines?"

"I'll take fractions."

And that is why I love my little guy.

Lessons were held in the casita. A full day of school and then a couple hours with me. My student worked hard.

"Jill, can you please get me a glass of water?"

"Why can't you get it yourself? The refrigerator is four feet from where you're sitting."

"Bonita always gets it for me when I ask."

"Bonita is not here. Get up and pour your own water. And while you're at it, I'll have one too."

Lessons were not always textbook. They were of life and reality…and old gals who were born, raised, and educated in New York City were the absolute perfect teachers to instruct about the real world.

Some evenings when Andrew had no one to play with, he'd mosey down to the casita to "hang." I taught him the word and encouraged him to be comfortable popping in just to discuss life, politics, and his trials on the school playground. He opened up to me, and I listened without being judgmental.

He loved Gypsy and on occasion snuggled *under* the casita table with the pup on his lap. He would read the classics to her, stopping now and then for me to help him with difficult words. One evening we *both* were under the casita kitchen table. Footsteps shuffled the walkway pebbles, followed by the familiar greeting, "Permission to approach?" Kep opened the door, initially couldn't spot us, and when he did, stood absolutely still.

"You did say you were an untraditional teacher, Jill. I wonder why we never did that background check." His face formed neither a smile nor a frown. A blank look took up the entire real estate of expression.

"Is there something you wanted, Kep?"

"We're heading to the beach in thirty minutes for mimosas and a snack. We'd like you to come."

"Sounds great. We'll be done shortly and will meet you by the main gate."

Andrew's dad spun around and shuffled back up to the main house. The scene was never mentioned, although I can only imagine what he was thinking.

Andrew was not permitted to wear pants with elastic waists. The family was extremely health conscious and would check his weight to be sure he stayed fit.

"Jill, I'm hungry. Can I have bread and jam?" he asked at the beginning of one class.

"Andrew, your parents don't want you snacking on anything other than fruit. There's fruit in the fridge. Help yourself."

"That's not going to do it today. *Please* can I have *one* piece of bread with jam?" He was already up making it. I let the discussion drop, and he sat to my right and opened his workbook. Footsteps down the casita path meant he'd be caught eating, so without the least bit of guilt, he slid the paper plate with bread and jam right over to my side of the table.

"Hey, don't put that *here*. Your parents already think I'm fat." In a split second, the bread with jam hit the floor, where Gypsy was happy to scoop it up.

Irina noticed Andrew's face. "Were you eating something pink?"

"Nope," he lied without hesitation. His mother looked at me, and I just shrugged. She stayed a minute and left.

"You owe me big time, kiddo," I said with a half smile.

"I know. Thank you." His eyebrows were raised like he had just escaped from a bank robbery.

And that's how a third grader and a senior citizen tutor bond.

Bonita generally did the run to pick up Andrew from the schoolyard. One day I offered to go. While the schoolyard was six feet below a stone wall, with a soccer ball under my arm, I scaled down the incline to meet him. Andrew's face painted a picture of question, but tossing the soccer ball to him satisfied his doubt. Several little classmates joined in and, speaking only in Spanish, said I was cool to play with them. One added that I stunk at soccer, but I smiled nonetheless.

Making the three-mile run to the little Spanish school became a part of the day I so enjoyed. About 90% of the time, Andrew slid into the VW with a scowl about how Jose or another bud did him wrong. It was during the fifteen-minute drive home that the grandmother in me stepped up to the plate. By the time we passed through the main gate, my little man was smiling and animated. Those were the times I thanked God for giving me the right words to make a child's heart happy.

# The Lessons, a Tad Off-Center...

Magic markers work great on windows and glass doors. A slider transforms into a blackboard, and something about writing where you are not supposed to, brings creativity and focused lessons. Just finishing some geometry on the windows, Andrew's dad approached the casita.

"*What* is this? We do *not* write on windows," he said like a drill sergeant.

"Why not? It wipes right off." I felt like I had to defend my methods.

"Andrew has had tutors before. They did not teach like this," he said rather gruffly.

"And they're not here any longer, are they? Your son is learning, is not bored, and stays focused. You yourself said he bounces into the house after being tutored for hours."

"Jill "

"Yes?"

"Never mind." Kep left, and I figured I'd be on an Iberian flight within the next twenty-four hours. But the man was an end-results guy and saw improvement in his son's ability. The methods were a tad off-center, admittedly, but brought successful results.

I was still employed.

The workbook we used depicted a series of pictures clearly fertilizing a story about a child in a schoolyard who had no one to play with. There was a drawing of a school, a teacher, a mournful little girl, and two children talking.

"Andrew, tell me what's happening on this page. Look closely at the pictures, put them in order, and tell me the story."

"Well, I see a barracks and a sergeant. The little girl was just told her father was being deployed and she was depressed. The other girl is trying to make her feel better."

"Holy moly. What makes you think that's a barracks? Could it be a school?"

"No. Look at the flag. It's probably the beginning of WWII." Andrew continued the story, and my mouth stayed ajar. This child was creative, smart, and totally untraditional.

Andrew wrote a story about a nursing home with a long-term resident everyone called Ma. One day Ma slipped in the parking lot when a relative came to take her out for the day. She hit her head on a car, and the police were called. When the officers spotted Ma, they concluded that's where the word *karma* originated (Car Ma).

My third-grade student was well traveled. Because his family had residences on multiple continents, words like Seychelles and Warsaw were injected into his stories. He would interject information about snakes with something along these lines: "When we were in Thailand…" or, "When we spent the month in Iceland…" Nothing like a third grader in America, Andrew's experiences offered him enormous benefits over other children.

During moments of trampoline play, I shouted directives he had to complete.

"Give me a verb, adverb, and two flips." He loved performing and was practicing language arts without realizing it.

When the weather warmed, Andrew perched himself on top of the water slide. Before he could splash into the pool, I called out new vocabulary words.

"What does *mandate* mean?" He'd yell out the definition and dash down the slide. Practicing vocabulary like this became a game he loved playing.

Computer programs were Andrew's favorite. He learned the location of all fifty states in two days. The educational website timed the students, and he and I would play until he finally beat me. The extraordinary competitive streak he had channeled most lessons into contest mode.

My little man was just plain fun to teach.

# Just Say *No*...

There lived on Ibiza the "dreaded" book club. Both Irina and Kep were members, and for some sadistic reason they repeatedly "suggested" I download the book and be prepared to partake in the two-and-a-half-hour literary discussion. First month the mandated book had to do with Muslim invasion around the times of the Crusades.

"Irina, I'm so sorry. I have nothing to download the book onto," I pleaded my case.

"Oh, Jill. We just ordered you an iPad. We will download it for you, and then we can all join in. This month the meeting is right over the mountain in Cala Longa. It should be fun."

Dear friends,

There is nothing "fun" about a book club, especially when it deals with a subject I have no interest in. Hate when someone gives me homework, and a book club *is* homework. I'd rather put my thumbs in a pencil sharpener.

The following month, Irina approached me again.

"Jill, we are hosting the book club here at our house. We are downloading this month's pick for you."

"Irina, thank you for thinking of me and including me in everything. I simply have no interest in reading a book and then discussing it with folks I never met."

The lady of the house pivoted and in less time than it takes to floss the pearly whites, she returned with a fully downloaded book about the events leading up to the start of WWI. God help me.

Every moment both parents had their noses in their Kindles. Mom was a determined soul and finished a day before the meeting. Dad was actually comical. He'd pretended to read it in front of his wife, then shut the device off and mumbled how much he hated the "damn book club." The day of the meeting, I took the VW and left for parts unknown. Joining a book club and sipping arsenic are on the same plane. Don't do either, and life will be good.

Irina is fit. Period. Her knees can bend without creaking and she shares the balance ability of the flying Wallendas. Her 115 pounds don't stop.

"Jill, I had a great idea. I've signed us up for an easy hike. It's only 5K and begins tomorrow at nine sharp." Apparently she thought I needed to burn calories. Or have a heart attack.

Oh goody. A hike on rocky terrain. I envisioned broken tibias and a puddle full of tears. What could be better?

We drove more than thirty minutes to the base of a mountain, where fourteen fat-free folks were milling about. They looked like a box of linguini decked out in full climbing gear.

"Irina, this is not a good idea. I'm the oldest and have no poles or anything appropriate for this. Why don't *you* go and I'll meet you here in three hours."

"Absolutely not," she replied. "You can do this!"

An attempt to navigate a mountain was number 756 on my list of things I ever wanted to do. Pulling out my fingernails was number 755.

Dicey beginning up steep, pebbled paths. Borrowed an extra pair of walking sticks that initially gave me stability and later were used as imaginary spears aimed at Irina. We turned a corner on the mountain to come to a set of boulders about three stories high. The hike leader fell to the back of the group to give me verbal encouragement. "Jill, don't look down."

"Wait, are we climbing up these? Are you kidding me?" I asked incredulously. The smooth-sided rocks hung over the sea. No railing. No flat area. I stared at Irina. I think I used the *F* word.

"Next week's walk will be easier, Jill. I have a good feeling about that."

"Forget it, Princess. You're on your own."

# My *One* Spanish Lesson...

I rina expected lessons to come to her rather than her driving to town. Each day either an aerobics instructor, yoga teacher, or TM woman rang at the stately gate. She especially enjoyed the transcendental meditation gal, who originally hailed from India but now called Ibiza home. Navya was about forty years old, more limber than a box of rubber bands, and changed her clothing and overall appearance depending on her mood. Traditional female sari could adorn her spectacular body on Tuesday but Thursday may bring the replica of a string bikini. A red dot stared back at me, drawn, painted, glued to the bridge of her nose. Never really figured out how that remained adhered despite whatever position she maneuvered her body into. Sometimes it was a darker, deeper red, other times I suppose the ink or whatever wore off.

The first time I met Navya, I bowed. Not sure why. Maybe I thought she was Asian, maybe it was just her exotic look. She did not return the bow. She did not smile. She did not invite me to the TM class. She sashayed by me like I was invisible.

The family thought my Spanish could use some tweaking. They hired Alondra, who instead of practicing conversational Spanish with the tutor should be donning the cover of a fashion magazine. The girl was gorgeous and gracious. Her smile revealed brilliant white teeth and a sincere desire to teach her native language.

Folks in Ibiza speak Castilian Spanish. The "ci" and "ce" have a "th" sound. Think *lisp*.

"Senora, Jill. Digame un estoria. Usa solo Espanol." (Tell me a story in Spanish.)

In my best Spanish I created a story of a lady bear leaving her hometown after her "boyfriend bear" was released from prison. They set up a drug lab in the woods. She eventually left him and went back to her little village to live a respectable life.

Alondra let a weak smile grow on her face. She slid off the teak porch chair and told me the lesson was over. She was always too busy to return for the next session.

# Some Facts and Questions...

Hard water wrecks your hair.
Mailing a letter to the States takes ten days and costs three dollars.

Most beaches are clothing-optional.

No shopkeepers speak English.

You can occupy a café seat for hours buying a single cup of coffee.

Dogs are welcomed in shops and restaurants.

Centipedes are the size of New Hampshire.

Ibiza residents speak a minimum of three languages.

Salt is a staple used in excess at every meal.

The number one surgery of Russian women living on Ibiza is leg extensions.

ISIS is more a nuisance in Ibiza than a threat.

Sneakers are taboo. High heels or leather sandals on all women are the order of the day.

No slacks or capris. It's leggings under a colorful tunic.

What do I miss I thought I could live without? Mac and cheese and Moody.

Is there any fear involved? None at all.

How do I feel about having no control? Damn good. All my needs are taken care of.

What is the most frustrating? Not knowing what's on the agenda until five minutes before.

Did my Spanish improve? Not sure. Maybe.

Biggest takeaway? This family is kind and gracious. Genuine. Fun. Generous.

What would you do differently now that you've been there? Nothing. It's perfect.

# The Family Is Coming...Call the Flamethrowers

I rina has a close family, mostly female. They spend eight weeks visiting the Ibizan compound, flying in from mainland Europe as well as the States. Included are grandchildren, nieces, sisters, brothers-in-law, and even larger extended family. They are guests of Irina and Kep, who couldn't be happier hosting their clan.

Two parties are orchestrated during the two months the compound is overflowing with relatives. Event-makers invite flamethrowers, belly dancers, stilt walkers, and jugglers. The grounds are decorated in silk, and exquisite sofas are strategically placed about the patios.

Two bands are in residence: a local Spanish trio with indigenous music and a hip group with electronic sounds that Ibiza is famous for. Much of, but not all, the sounds are in synch with the laser beams darting across the pool. Colorful, bright rays jump about the perimeter of the saltwater pool, an addition Kep ordered directly from the Disney Paris folks.

Professional grill masters turn the pig and lamb, marinate the steaks, and offer their services to the guest chefs hired for the day.

Floral arrangements, enormous displays of exotic flora, frame the venue and help spread the scent of flowers. Invisible spritzers send off their own aromas.

The festivities last all day, and everyone in town, and probably on the island, hope they are invited.

One of my favorite relatives was Mika, thirty-five years old, single, and full of vitality. She had a background in dance and on occasion heading to main meal, she would belt out a tune and choreograph it with a pirouette and some leg kicks. High on life, Mika *was* a party. Outspoken, she'd share her point of view whether or not it was requested. Unfortunately, immediately prior to landing in Ibiza, she'd spent time in the Caribbean, where she contracted the Zika virus. After three full days in a horizontal position, sipping chicken soup and water, Mika finally emerged from the guest wing. For eight weeks, our days were in entertainment mode with her zany routines. The kids called her Mika with Zika and chucked endlessly each time they heard the rhyme.

The guest area was an addition to the main house, with outside entrance, private bath, and large teak shutters. Decorated professionally, it became home to various family members as they shuffled on and off the compound.

As more and more family arrived, it became apparent a nanny would have to be added to the mix.

An ad placed on a website in mainland Europe introduced the family to Vivienne, a French girl with dimples the size of Paris. Irina interviewed her via Skype, and three days later she sat at main meal, feeling out her niche inside this cosmopolitan clan.

Each member of the family brought a distinct personality. All slim to the extreme, each arrival made me feel brick loads larger. Healthy, dark hair, long enough to sit on, was part of the commonality of all the women, and the ability to sit perfectly upright all through main meal apparently was part of their genes. Two hours without leaning back or relaxing was an impossible task for me, and while they were poised like royalty, I was the frumpy American.

*Dear Diary,*

*Is there a school where they teach how to sit up perfectly straight without making a chiropractic appointment? There are no elbows on the table. Everyone drinks wine during the day. They can finish up with specialty coffee and nothing to dunk in it. Why does Kep ask if I want seconds?*

*Note to self: try out the gym*

Having a nanny makes children disappear. One day she dressed them as pirates, donned in professional costumes, and hosted a pirate party in the full-size pirate ship created when Andrew was born. Every detail of the ship was authentic, Kep previously having hired people to purchase appropriate items to adorn the buccaneer vessel.

One afternoon the nanny and I taught the children to make piñatas. The mixture of flour and water, newspaper strips, and inflated balloons created a sticky mess on one of the picnic tables. Kep strolled by with a video camera. "This *mess* will be cleaned up, yes?" he said to all of us. His eyes locked on mine. "Yes?"

He turned and left. I felt like a schoolgirl being singled out by the principal.

An hour after the project ended, I was still washing down the picnic table decorated with large splashes of papier-mâché.

*Dear Diary,*

*This is the first time I spied another side of Kep. Stern. Bossy. I wonder if there's a dungeon on the compound somewhere.*

*Note to self: Call Mike. Remind him where the safe deposit key is.*

The nanny and I became compadres, both being "the help." A distinction was obvious, however: the times I was invited out to restaurants and outings, or for champagne on the north porch, and repeatedly asked if there was anything they could do to make my stay more comfortable. Vivienne noticed the attention, and in the privacy of my casita she pulled up a chair and asked me about it. There really was no explanation. Many times the family treated me like I was a guest rather than an employee. Changing the subject, my new friend and I chatted about life. One afternoon, when we were both off, we hopped in the VW and set off to grab a coffee in another town. Maybe it was she being thirty years younger than I or maybe the disparity of Europeans to Americans, but relationships she encountered and those of my generations were 180 degrees apart. Not sure whether I envied or pitied her.

Vivienne was still working for the family when I took a break in early summer. We keep in touch on Facebook.

*Dear Diary,*

*I really like Vivienne. She is so footloose and thinks so differently than I do. Not sure it's the generation or the American/European thing. She tells me her sex life is a 50. What number is mine? Is it even in the double digits?*

Some things in life you just can't make up. Like an old gal with self-proclaimed ADHD being perfectly content to spend the day on just four acres. Walled.

Silent. With mountain views and the sole rant of a rooster reverberating off the hillside. Certainly this must be heaven. I don't deserve this Mediterranean nirvana.

Dear friends,

Dad moseyed down to casita with specialty coffee and recap of lesson. Says his son bounded into main house to tell him how well he did with me.

"What did you do, Jill, to make an eight-year-old so excited about learning?"

It's called thirty years in the classroom, but I just smiled and didn't add any dialogue.

It was Monday...the busy-ness of life to reset its cycle.

Wind up the compound because who knows *what* will happen. What unfamiliar cars will beep through the fortress gate, tagging along more gym equipment or ten huge totes of fresh vegetables/fruits? Meat? Well, that could be carried in the chef's pocket, if Mom is in charge. But...Mom's out of the country. Dad's in charge. Probably expected are ten totes of steak and pork chops followed by a single stalk of celery!

# Posing the Question...

B ecause sunset didn't arrive until ten p.m., it was not uncommon for my lessons to be in the evening. Finished up one night and my charge bolted from the casita, and before I could pour a cup of chamomile, his dad dropped in. Two hours later, Kep departed, leaving my jaw ajar.

"Jill, you know how Andrew responds to you. He's learning and rarely complains about coming to you for lessons. Irina and I were wondering if you would consider staying on until the end of the year. Right now we're anticipating being in Europe, but we may relocate to our Pebble Beach, California, home. Of course you would have your own accommodations there. If we are still in Europe in November, we shall take you to the Christmas markets in Germany." He paused. A very long pause. Then the pressure: "Can you make that commitment to us?"

My head was spinning. Mike was home holding down the fort. Moody would wonder where his mom was, and my grandchildren...

"Let me think about it," I began. "This was supposed to be a three-month position, and that's actually one of the only reasons I considered it in the first place."

Kep nodded, smiled, and flashed a wink. Whenever he did that it meant there was a surprise attached.

*Dear Diary,*

*I'm invited to spend more time in heaven, but I have obligations on earth. What path to tread. Andrew is doing so well, the family is a delight. Ibiza is spectacular. I'm feeling indecisive…like a game show contestant choosing door number one or what's behind the curtain.*

*You never know where your life will take you. Who on earth thought I'd hop a plane to work in Europe? Who even thought I'd hop a plane in the first place? I hate flying.*

*Dear Lord, please show me your plan. And hoping it includes chocolate.*

Dear friends,

I'm invited to lengthen my stay. Can I do it? I miss hearing American news. I miss a radio. I miss Dollar Stores and girlfriends. The dad has become a friend, but a male friend is not the same as a girlfriend.

Sometimes I look at the world like a missile, and other times like a clamshell. Some days the atmosphere has parameters and omits the coziness of boundaries.

The days where life is a clamshell are comforting but at the same time limiting. Safe. Secure. Maybe just boring. Ball and chain. Unfulfilling. As the finiteness of life becomes more apparent, I crave the missile effect. Open wide. Seize the opportunities, double the vitamin B12.

# The Spectacular Medieval Fair...

Ibiza has an annual medieval fair. Because the actual architecture is still standing, the cathedral on the mountaintop, the buildings centuries old, you can easily believe you've been transported to a time of jesters and public hangings. Aroma of food appropriate of the period wafted across the stone courtyards. Elders dressed in medieval garb served treats and paraded about the ancient, narrow roadways. Vendors under animal skin tents illuminated their period wares with candlelight, shrouding the handmade crafts with an orange-tan hue. The area became an open-air theater filled with chocolate makers, artisans, silversmiths, and spice traders.

We climbed the cobblestone steps and slipped silently into the church. The churches had a dual purpose; as much as a religious need, the structures held refuge for locals during Turkish invasions. They therefore had defense towers.

"I wish I could get the enthusiasm you have, Jill. But I've traveled and lived around the whole world, and it is hard to get excited anymore," lamented Kep.

He continued his previous thought. "But watching your face and how moved you are makes me rethink this venue of history."

Night had fallen and we stood against an ancient stone wall to ingest the spirit of Ibiza Town. The lights danced on the mountainside as well as on the illuminated mega-yachts moored in the harbor. They painted a portrait of majesty. I cried. Muffled but obvious. Andrew looked perplexed. Kep smiled. "I don't deserve this magical night," I whispered.

*Dear Diary,*

*Can this be real? Why on earth was I chosen to experience what life is like on the other side of the tracks?*

*Love it here but wish it were possible to transport my family/friends to this mountain of bliss standing proudly right in the Mediterranean. Reminds me of a king's throne framed by his palace.*

Dear friends,

Thundering reverberation of the Roman chariots against the thousand-year-old walls. Cobblestone roads still etched where the carts flew by now displaying the period garb adorned by the locals of Ibiza. It is Medieval Night on the Rock.

*Se Vende*, for sale signs in the windows of the narrow stone streets. People still live here, in flats hundreds of years old. Mostly Muslim now, there are still signs of the Jewish sections and underground entrances to the Christian churches banned in antiquity.

Four of us arrived in Ibiza Town about seven p.m. Grabbed a tapas of goose liver and eel and, although that sounds questionable, it was downright fabulous.

Dad offered his arm for balance and support in climbing to the top of the castle that shared the pinnacle with a church. Cannot, with limited writing talent, express the beauty of this cathedral in the clouds. Overlooked the harbor with its blanket of yachts.

Stopped in a Moroccan tent to sip mint tea. Their music was belting out unusual tunes by local Moroccans. Dark hair, large brown eyes, wrinkled carving of life on their faces. No one spoke English.

Left the tent to capture the rest of this enormous fair. Acres and acres of ancient architecture alive with perfect recreations of vendors and their wares.

A reborn period of European history, and I was privy to take part.

Open-fire donut bakers and cider stirrers did their thing in local attire. The scent of warmed apples and sugared cakes wafted across the cobblestone.

The family was amusing. They enjoyed attending every festival and fair. Not once did they prefer passing on what could be construed as a good time. On a moment's notice, they packed up their family and little Gypsy and headed out.

Dogs are welcomed at just about every event on Ibiza. They are in restaurants and on beaches. They shop with their owners, and often the shopkeepers bring their dogs to work with them.

Gypsy accompanied us everywhere we went. She was well-behaved, absolutely adorable, and obviously loved. Her partner in crime, the resident cat was her best buddy. Despite Kep's resounding demand that the feral cat was not to be fed, Irina had a stash of cat food hidden, which she offered to the feline twice daily. Andrew must have been in on it, because those times when Irina was out of the country, the cat still had his meals.

"You see? The cat looks healthy," said Kep. "That means he is finding mice like he should. I told you we do not need to feed him!" No one said a word to divulge the "secret." Least of all me.

Kep left the compound, country, and continent often. He thoughtfully returned with delectable chocolate for the tutor.

# Imposed Limitations...the Shoe Drops

O ne evening after I finished lessons, Kep called out his usual greeting. "Permission to approach?" He grabbed the kitchen chair and the conversation began like this:

"Jill, I have 400 people working for me." Where is this going? I thought. "So are you saying you now have 399?"

"Oh *no*! We want you here and we love how Andrew is responding to you. But we are strict with him, and I already mentioned to you that using a computer is not how we want him taught."

"Listen, Kep. Don't tell me how to teach. He *has* to use a computer. That is nonnegotiable. Period. Why don't you go perform surgery on someone? And don't use a scalpel." Those were words worthy of job termination, but the connection that had blossomed between my student and me was worth advocating for. I crossed the line and awaited the repercussions.

Kep jumped up abruptly and headed for the door. His body spun to make eye contact. "He is *not* to use a computer!"

"He *is* going to use a computer. And by the way, he needs a new one."

*Dear Diary,*

*Today was a turning point. My profession was criti-*
*cized and I was rude to my employer. If I'm to ready*
*this little boy for American schools, he* must *be familiar*
*with computers. Period. Should I start packing? Will*
*tomorrow bring my airline ticket back to the States?*
*What will I tell my friends when I return early? Should*
*I apologize to the dad? Do I teach the way someone*
*tells me to…or teach the way I know is right?*

*Dear God, this child has become so special. Help*
*me not let him down.*

The phone in the casita sounded shrilly ten minutes
later when Kep dialed me. "OK. He can use a computer.
But I want him using a pen as well."

"Fair enough. He'll use a pen to write you a note on
how much he loves his new computer."

The phone went dead.

# Mother Dearest Was Correct...

When you visit a foreign country in vacation mode, you generally move about. But when you're *living* there for three months, you need to get a haircut, change the car oil, and get a pedicure. The foreign country suddenly morphs into "home." You become more reflective and retrieve memories you initially believed were useless. Snuggled in bed last night, exhausted, my down comforter framed my thoughts with "aha!" moments. My mother came to mind, with wagging index finger and a list of things I needed to know in life. She was right. And when her lectures began, they always set foot out of the gate with: "You never know where your life is going to take you. Be prepared. Know what to do. Understand protocol and dream *big*." If she could see me now.

Dinner table etiquette is paramount. It tells your tablemates who you are. Bread dish always to your left. Break, not cut, bread. Pick up the smaller piece and eat it. Never the entire roll. Move butter from central dish to your bread dish before buttering your bread. Cut your food into small bites, never allowing a piece of *anything* to be dangling from your mouth. Don't reach across the table, but rather ask for the item politely. Make eye contact with the server, thanking him/her.

"Mom, you were right on the money. You simply do not know where you will find yourself later in life."

# The Doctor Is In...

Having a resident MD is a plus. Convenient.
"Kep, I had a charley horse last night. Twice. Any
idea what that could be from?"

"What is a charley horse?"

As healthy as I try to keep with eating right and a
Walgreen's shelf of supplements, a virus stopped at the
casita and drove me between the sheets. The family
knew I was under the weather and gave me privacy.
Except for Kep.

"Permission to approach?" He slightly pushed the
casita door, poked his head in, and stopped dead in
his tracks.

"You look like shit."

As ill as I felt, he still made me laugh.

"Is that a professional term?"

A pivot and some mumbling, and he was gone.
About twenty minutes later, he returned with a mug
of hot chicken soup. Thoughtful. Sweet. Sat up in bed
and sipped slowly.

For some reason, this brilliant physician, businessman, husband, and father began a soliloquy on
eighth-century European invasions. My head was

pounding and my angry bowels moaning. Patience was limited.

"You talk too much," I said matter-of-factly.

"What do you mean? You always sound so inquisitive."

"Give me the abridged version."

"This *is* the abridged version."

*Dear Diary,*

*Manhattan and Ibiza share the same sky. How is it possible that Broadway's neon lights and the solitude of an island compound marvel at the same moon?*

*Why aren't I homesick? Is it because I'm being treated like a princess? Is it because my student is so much fun to teach? Is it because my employer just bought me a bike?*

# More Change...New Work Hours

My employers altered my hours. Andrew was officially off for the summer from the little Spanish school, and I would be homeschooling him using an American curriculum. Four hours daily and weekends off. Began immediately and found that beginning at ten a.m. and finishing up at right before main meal worked out well for everyone.

The family constantly changed plans. Actually, no one *made* plans, because at any given moment, a relative would appear, bag and baggage, to announce he/she would spend a month or so on the compound. Without notice, Irina could be seen leaving for the airport and Kep could be called to a business meeting in Hawaii or China. *Change*...it's what made this job so fascinating.

Dear friends,

My work hours are altered. Like the schedule very much. Weekends off and have more time with my new British friends. A pitcher of sangria helped me slip out of the white beach chair and onto my feet. It was

Sunday and that meant dancing at the sea. I'm here seven weeks and this place is still special.

Mom, niece, daughter out on the town. Nanny is watching three-year-old and older children frolic in the pool. And announcement from Kep: "All of you. Be ready in forty-five minutes. No reminders. We're going to a restaurant. If you aren't at the gate on time, you stay home with the nanny." Everyone appeared in front of the fortress entrance as the heavy beams slid open.

# A Surprise for the Tutor...

## (Ahoy, Matey)

It was a Thursday, the end of June. Andrew being finished with school left plenty of time for "casita lessons." And chat. And bonding.

"Jill. Don't make any plans for this afternoon. My parents have a surprise for you."

"What *kind* of surprise?"

"Can't tell you. Just don't make plans."

Less than thirty minutes later, Irina strolled into the casita.

"We have an outing planned for today, Jill. Kep arranged it himself because he thinks you will really enjoy it. I agree. So you'll need swimwear, sunscreen, and a change of clothes. Please be ready to leave in twenty minutes."

A change of clothes through my middle-class eyes is the phrase for "We're going somewhere fancy." No further information. No idea how long the outing would be. Was the whole family going? Bringing swimwear meant "bad hair day" and a change of clothes meant you need to pull yourself together after said "bad hair day."

Three cars of family members, plus the nanny, and we were on our way. Long ride. Didn't recognize the final destination other than a harbor with mega-yachts moored aside their dinghy.

Almost hidden among the sleek, modern watercraft stood proud an eighty-eight-foot perfect replica of an old wooden pirate ship!

Irina took my hand, gave me a squeeze, and pointed to the boat. "This is how you will spend your last day on Ibiza. But you promised you'd be back in September, right?"

Without thinking, I threw my arms around her dainty body and sobbed. Uncontrollably. "Irina, I cannot repay you for all you do for me."

"You *have* paid us, Jill. Our son has learned so much. He is very fond of you, and you brought life and fun to our home. You owe us nothing more."

The vessel was enormous. Aft to forward seemed like an endless corridor of lines and sails and heavy wooden cranks.

The crew of three made us comfortable with drinks and snacks and offered us cabins in which to change. Each room had a private bathroom. Red terry cloth foam beds under canvas canopies invited protection from the glaring sun and a respite of cool breezes. Splendid. Incredible. Memory-making.

The captain threw down an anchor and the whole lot of us made an immediate exit. Kids screamed and laughed, with scissor kicks and somersaults while adults dove gracefully. The tutor held the ladder and gingerly slipped into the emerald water. A fire drill approach to the water like an exodus of students on their last day of school. Emotionally on overdrive, a little bite of my bottom lip kept me from tears.

We all hit gears with proper clothing to be dropped at the dock of an exclusive restaurant. No windows, just openings as large as castle doorways, all over-looking the blue-gem waters.

The meal was mediocre, ironically, for the cost. But the forty-two euro ice cream dessert, served in an iced bucket with a buffet of toppings on each table, was unique, and so large the family could not finish it.

Picked up from the dock to head back to pirate ship. Spent another few hours sunning and swimming then finally headed home.

Slept like a drugged poet, with a smile on my heart and a thousand scenes dancing in my mind.

This family is special.

*Dear Diary,*

*Ibiza is calling, and I must return.*

Dear friends,

I will be returning to Ibiza in September. Hoping to connect with all of you the month I'll be home. The magical island is only surpassed by the adorable student I'm teaching and the fabulous family with whom I'm living.

Don't deserve these blessings but infinitely grateful I met them along my path.

# Bidding Adieu

B ittersweet hugs to everyone as I grabbed my bags for what would be a long journey home.

"Jill, I am going to miss you with all my heart," cried my student as he buried his face in my shoulder. "Do you promise you will come back?"

"Andrew. You won't be getting off lessons that easily. Of course I'll be back. We'll pick up where we left off." I looked into his eyes with my hand holding his chin. He was so special to me. "Have a good summer vacation in Greenland. You can tell me all about it when I come back." A squeeze and hug, and it was time to board the Mercedes "shuttle" Kep used as a pet name for his SUV.

Cannot recall one single conversation I shared with my employer during the forty-minute ride to the tiny Ibiza Airport.

Nonverbal communication of appreciation on both sides and a silent acknowledgment that we'd become friends.

Iberian Airlines has a policy that for five hundred euros you can upgrade to first class if it's done *at* the airport within two hours of departure. Otherwise, the cost is four thousand euros! And so, for a little more than five hundred dollars, I enjoyed the privacy of a cubby with bed, movies, music, and culinary delights. The food that was passed around before departure appeared to be the main meal, and not realizing it was just the starters, I swallowed the one sleeping pill I'd packed for flying. Awoke right before landing in Miami, where Mike was anxiously awaiting his lady.

The fantasy was over. A dream that may never have happened.

Maneuvered our car across six lanes of Miami traffic and pulled into our driveway two hours later.

*Dear Diary,*

*What just happened?*

# Summer in South Florida

S ince I knew I was returning to Ibiza, the short time in the Sunshine State had to be packed with get-to-gethers with friends and family. Flew to New York and then Kentucky to share hugs with my sons and grandchildren. Booked and enjoyed a cruise before heading to the North Carolina mountains to kidnap some cooler temps. Unfortunately, two weeks in a charming mountain cabin brought us more 90-degree discomfort. No escaping the heat.

The normally stress-free summer in South Florida was anything but. Still reeling from the experiences I'd been offered and anxious about the ones yet to cross my path.

I caught myself in a spending frenzy, no doubt from seeing how much money my employers shelled out. Only their tax returns and mine didn't even share the same galaxy. Curtailed the spending and settled again into middle class. The challenge to forget the family and all the memorable experiences intensified rather than diminished. They had a profound effect on me, and the way they treated me saturated my soul with gratitude.

The calendar seemed to turn its own pages. Before we knew it, Mike was helping me pack for the second chapter in Ibiza.

# Second Time Around...

T aking another step into paradise knowing full well what to expect erased undue anxiety. I thought. A pound of anticipation replaced fear sort of like knowing a new school year was approaching in a school you were familiar with. Even with some butterflies in your belly, you're over-the-moon excited to continue the adventure.

How would it be different? What facets would be the same? Would I remember how to get to all the nearby towns? Would my British friends be available to socialize? How would my student react to my return?

My luggage was packed with items I knew were expensive on the Rock. Brought more appropriate clothing and fewer vitamin supplements. Ran around shadowed by cups of caffeine, short-tempered and with a feeling of too much to do and not enough time to accomplish everything before making the trek to Miami International Airport at the end of the week.

Standing with Mike in our kitchen, my heart began to race. A piercing, darting pain felt like a skullcap compressing my head. The vision in my left eye disappeared, and despite repeatedly blinking, I could not correct the darkness. Instinctively, I reached out to grasp the quartz countertop and froze in fear.

"I need to call the doctor. I can't see out of my left eye," I cried to Mike.

"I think you should go to the emergency room. This seems serious," he replied, not really knowing what to do.

Raced six miles to the ER hospital entrance. My blood pressure was dangerously high and I was diagnosed as having had a retina stroke. A piece of plaque dislodged, blocking blood flow. The medical term is central retinal vein occlusion.

Admitted to the hospital and remained for two days until blood pressure was controlled. Appointments were made for cardiologist, retina specialist, and myriad other physicians before I was permitted to leave the country. The fact that the flight was so long concerned more than one doctor, but I finally got the green light to proceed.

Salt was eliminated from my diet. One cup of caffeine daily permitted, the rest, chamomile only. All stress had to be avoided, and an increase in medication was now on the dance card.

Discharged from the hospital and knowing you'd be flying the day after next to Ibiza, Spain, makes one crazy. Prayed, meditated, and tried to convince myself that the vision would eventually return. Not sure how to describe how scary it was to see through only one eye.

Mike and I managed to pilot the Honda to Miami. We hugged and I boarded the Iberian flight my confidence now enveloped in doubt. The attempt to relax was for naught, and while a shadow of sight had briefly reappeared, it now traveled back to complete darkness.

I nestled into my seat and talked to God.

*Dear Diary,*

*This is awful. What happens if my other eye goes dark? I'll be totally blind! Will I be able to maneuver around the house? How will I walk Moody? What effect will sight loss have on my relationship with Mike?*

# The Tutor Arrives for Chapter Two...

An uneventful flight through Madrid accompanied the one-hour jaunt from mainland Spain to Ibiza. Slept a bit on board, but the satchels under my eyes contradicted my insistence that I was rested.

"Oh my God!" cried Kep. "What happened to you?"

"Good to see you too, Kep. Where's your better half and Andrew?"

"Irina is out of town." That could mean hanging her hat in another country, but more likely it was on another continent. "Andrew's in school." He paused to stare into my eyes, a grin growing from the side of his mouth. "We are really happy you made it back." His greeting was genuine, and he had no way of knowing only one eye could focus on his face. He grabbed three pieces of luggage from the cart I had piled them on before passing through customs, and with a sprint I could hardly keep up with, he threw them into the back of the Mercedes SUV.

We were on our way. Chapter two of an adventure I'll never forget.

A déjà vu of the airport-to-compound drive just six months earlier was 180 degrees different this time. No anxiety. No unknown. A reconnection with a friend, some laughter, and the invisible curtain that kept us in a more formal mode was now gone. While I was still the employee, this time around would be much more comfortable. I'd hoped.

The Mercedes pulled through the gates just after Bonita had picked up Andrew from school. My "little man" jumped out of the dusty red car and dashed to give me a hug. My throat had a lump, and I hugged him back. Bonita offered me a tight embrace, and while still in her arms, I peered into the sky to thank the Lord for another chance to make a difference in this child's life.

"You look a little different, Jill," remarked Andrew. "Are you tired from flying from America?"

"Are you referring to the saddlebags under the baby blues, sweetie?" He had no idea what that meant.

*Dear Diary,*

*Note to self: teach idioms*

# The Oktoberfest on a Gerbil Wheel...

A day and a half after flying from the States to Ibiza, and less than a week after being hospitalized with a retinal stroke, I readied for the flight off the Rock to hit the Oktoberfest in Munich. Bonita the house-keeper, cook, babysitter, and dedicated long-term help, kept Andrew. Irina was still out of the country, so the trip to mainland Germany was slotted for Kep and me. He booked two flights, two hotel rooms, and plenty of surprises for the tutor he had hired six months prior via Skype.

Europeans do not share the same protocol philoso-phies as Americans. They are more pragmatic, less con-cerned with social taboos, and much less inclined to think twice about a man and woman traveling together as friends. In this case, it was employer and employee, but it sort of fit the same rule. Irina had chosen to pass up the Oktoberfest but offered some good tips on how to maneuver through the largest fair on the planet.

Landed in Munich solo, as my employer had a previous business engagement in another city. Found my way through the Munich Airport, finally locating railway transportation to the inner city. The train ride took about forty-five minutes, giving me ample time to strike up conversations with fellow passengers. Most spoke no English, but one fellow who had previously lived in the States conversed like an American native.

"Do you happen to know where the Eurostars Grand Central Hotel is?" I asked him.

In the same time it takes to recite the Pledge of Allegiance *backward*, the German stranger finally figured out where the hotel was. Efficiency with a smart phone / GPS apparently was not his strong point. But kudos for the information, and when the trainman called my stop, I had confidence in where I was headed.

The spectacular hotel was reserved on my employer's credit card, but with the cost of the flight on him and all the food, I decided to pick up the hotel charges. That was probably the defining moment where I began to consider this a trip for friends rather than a perk of a job.

When you partake in the famed Oktoberfest, you are expected to dress the part. For weeks before passing through the entrance gate, an appropriate dirndl was designed and created using fabrics and notions purchased in the states. A seamstress in South Florida who speaks only Spanish sewed the pieces together using photos of what the finished product should look like. It was adorable. I thought. The third time Kepler asked if he could buy me a "real" dirndl, I began to feel it wasn't up to official Oktoberfest standards.

"Jill, here is a dirndl shop," he pointed out while strolling about Munich. "Why don't we get you one? You can pick out the color."

"Kep, the one I have is fine. It's a one-night event, and I'll never have an opportunity to wear it again." I paused. "How much are they anyway?"

"We can get one for 450 euros," he said nonchalantly.

"Almost five hundred dollars for a dress? For one night? Are you kidding?"

"I paid two thousand euros for my wife's dirndl. It is OK. Let's go in and find you something."

"Donate the money to an orphanage. I'm fine with what I have," I insisted.

In the next hour and a half, twice more Kep suggested my American dirndl be replaced. Each time I insisted what I had was fine. Although never mentioned again, I know he was disappointed that an "official" Oktoberfest dress was not adorning the woman who would be clinking beer mugs with him that evening.

When you travel with your employer and one whose background is European with different cultures and mores, an imaginary line is drawn. Do you have your own opinion or stay within the guideline of your boss?

Security at the Oktoberfest was extraordinary. Fears of terrorism prompted an overabundance of police presence. Even with obvious diligence, I could not help peering about for suspicious activity. Since most of those attending were inebriated, *all* the behavior looked suspicious. We were sober and, disappointingly, stayed that way all night.

The largest festival in the world lasts about seventeen days and begins the third Saturday in September. On the average, six million people enjoy the parades, rides, and of course the endless liters of beer, precariously juggled by rushing waitresses in bosom-enhanced dirndls. Bustling crowds belting out tunes in off-key voices surprised me by knowing all the words to the American songs. Surprisingly, not one German tune was on tap the entire time we visited each beer tent.

Reservations are a must to secure a seat in your tent of choice. If you're off the street, like we were, you grab what you can, cramped among strangers slurring their words, offering stories in their native German tongue, and otherwise hugging you with a sway and a smile. Sticky tables and floors, soft pretzels the size of a dinner plate and attitudes of devil-may-care are the tapestry for this famed festival.

Surprisingly, Kep fell back and let me lead to find us an available table spot. Not an easy task, even for this native New Yorker. In one tent and out another, we finally found a second-floor (with a great view of revelers) table that had two empty eighteen-inch spots on a sticky wooden bench. We did the best to communicate and slipped into our newly acquired (and temporary) real estate. A dirndl-clad waitress dashed over projectile-like to take our order, insuring no other wait staff would earn her tip. Some singing and chugging most, but not all, of the liter beer mug ushered us out the gate for a spectacular night.

Extending 164 feet into the night was a brightly illuminated Ferris wheel, the renowned icon of the folk fest.

"Let's go on the wheel," suggested Kepler.

"What? It's twenty-four euros each," I said incredulously. "That's ridiculous. Forty-eight dollars for one ride?"

We boarded and sat across from each other in the six-passenger enclosure. The panorama of the enormous structure rendered me speechless. Another scene I'd not be able to describe to friends back home.

How does one sketch a drawing of euphoria? Of a fantasy that materialized? You do what you can with words but keep the most profound images privately locked in your heart.

*Dear Diary,*

*I'm the oldest dirndl-clad festival "frau." I always believed Germans knew how to party, and seeing them dancing at the Oktoberfest confirms their proclivity to having a good time. I'm in heaven.*

We left the Oktoberfest sober, with full bellies trying in vain to digest combinations of heavy German food and delectable sweets. Grabbed the train, now filled with other traditional German lederhosen and dirndl-clad folks, and blended in appearance-wise but divulged a difference: we were speaking English.

An internal debate began, whether to welcome sleep or to digest the tapestry of loud German laughter and the smell of beer as the partygoers exhaled. The train ride was 360-degree entertainment...in surround sound.

"What do men wear under their leather shorts?" I nonchalantly posed to Kep. What are *you* wearing under *your* lederhosen?" Immediate regret as the question streamed from my lips.

"What?" His eyebrows raised, but nothing more was offered.

"I'm sorry. It's just that those lederhosen look so uncomfortable," I continued.

Kepler changed the subject without addressing my curiosity.

"Did you have a good time tonight? I have a surprise for you tomorrow," he added like a child offering his teacher a secret gift.

Still embarrassed by my personal question and wishing I had not been so forward, I offered a smile to confirm that the night was memorable.

Arrived at the spectacular hotel and I headed toward the elevator.

"Do you want to have a drink before heading upstairs?" Kep asked.

"I'm kind of beat. Think I'll pass, but thank you for the offer," I politely responded.

"What was it you enjoy, chamomile tea? I will order you one. Do you take lemon or drink it plain? Do you want something to go with it?"

I stood cemented in place, and within a nano-second, the situation reconfirmed I was "the help." The employee. And although treated like family or friend, my options were still limited.

"I'll take it with milk, please."

We found small tan leather seats across from each other and rested our drinks on a round glass table the size of a large Frisbee. For the next ninety minutes we covered ground on politics, education, and the role of China in the American economy. We talked about Andrew and New York City taxi drivers.

"Kep," I began, "you are very easy to talk with. I had the best time tonight and I am so grateful for how you and Irina have treated me. You are a very special family."

"It is our pleasure, Jill. You are good for our son, and we are glad you made it over to Europe." He smiled an impish grin. He took a few steps away from our little table and turned abruptly. "Yes, I am wearing underwear under my lederhosen." He strolled to the elevator and pressed the button, and without any more dialogue, we made our way upstairs. He walked me to my room.

"Kep..."I began, not really knowing what I was going to say.

He smiled, winked, and strolled on down to his own room.

*Dear Diary,*

*Are you kidding me?*

A text early the following morning; "Are you up? I will meet you downstairs for breakfast. Please do not take a lot of time. We have an appointment."

Showered and slipped on black jeans and a bright purple sweater with gold buttons the size of roast beef sandwiches. Golden hoop earrings with Egyptian engravings and a couple costume bangle bracelets, I headed down to breakfast.

"Oh my God, Jill. You look so....American. Do you have anything a little more, um, conservative?"

*Dear Diary,*

*Say what? This sweater is stunning...if you live in Vegas or New Jersey. Should I change my clothes or hold my ground?*

"Can you handle this outfit through breakfast, and I'll change before we head out?"

"I will wait for you. Why don't you go up now and find something more comfortable?"

Breakfasted with black sweater, black-and-white scarf, pearl stud earrings, and no bracelets. Lesson learned: gaudy is not appropriate anywhere other than South Florida.

# A Convertible through Bavaria...

A waiting us outside the hotel entrance was a white convertible with soft red leather seats and a dashboard surely designed by NASA. Kep opened the passenger door for me and bounded around to slip into the driver's seat. He adjusted the steering wheel and lowered the top. Late September breezes sent us on our way.

"Jill, this is your surprise. I am taking you to a special place. It is the castle where Irina and I got married. It's on an island, so we will be on a ferry later this afternoon. There is a restaurant there you will love. Are you ready?"

His eyes twinkled like a young boy earning the honor to lead the town parade.

*Dear Diary,*

*What did I do to deserve this?*

We sped through Bavaria on winding lanes lined with muraled chalets. Enormous window boxes, overflowing brightly colored floral blooms draped down hugging the storybook walls. Lush lawns, rolling gently like manicured fairways, blanketed the German region.

Temps in the high 60s, cloudless sky, and wonderland reality of dreams painted a portrait in my mind. A slice of fantasy that materialized; scenes you read about in novels.

Background music seeped from the radio, barely audible but securing a script in the play that was staged at the base of the Alps.

We drove about an hour, slowing dramatically when the quaint towns popped up around roadway curves. The scenes changed from knolled meadows to busy villages in a matter of seconds. White goats called to each other, and a lone cow seemed to be busy thinking about her life.

A sharp turn, Kep pulled into a parking lot, graveled, with tree logs situated horizontally as borders.

"Ready? We are here. You do not need to bring your purse. But you may want your jacket for when we are on the ferry."

Tossed my woolen cape over one shoulder, straightened out my neck scarf, adjusted my sunglasses, and followed the leader, the boss, the gentle man who would spend the next five hours reliving his spectacular wedding day. It was only nine years prior, and I wondered if to him it felt like decades ago.

The castle stood like the king who once inhabited it, tall and mighty. It was on an island that could clearly be seen from where we stood. Off to the side of the path waited a horse-drawn carriage where several people were scrunched together, leaving us little room. Kep helped me onto the rear wagon steps and groaned for effect.

"I heard that. Was that really necessary?" I asked, not actually expecting a response. His smile squinted his face until the blue of his eyes disappeared like a comedian entertained by his own jokes.

The wagon lurched forward, pitching the passengers back and forth like a choreographed routine. Rocks and ruts challenged the wooden wheels to offer a comfortable ride, but no one complained, and all seemed happy to be jostled about in this historical landscape.

Boarded the ferry surrounded by languages other than English. An exotic adventure, with international flair sketched a drawing I would not soon forget.

Imposing wooden doors fortified the castle, and as we approached its entrance, Kep spun around.

"This is where the magic took place, Jill." He gestured with a wave through the air. "It was a perfect evening. Irina looked stunning. She took my breath away." He paused, then added, "And still does."

The fountains and towering stone statues were framed by gardens, and I could only imagine how it appeared illuminated in the darkness of night. We strolled the island for another hour. I listened. Kep talked. Reminisced, really. There was some excitement in his voice but also a hint of something he preferred not to share with his son's tutor.

A late lunch, early dinner meal, outdoors on long, red-checkered tables, fertilized more conversation. Topics such as bee stings and flossing, proper mountain-climbing footwear, and where I learned to teach so untraditionally hastened the two-hour supper. Laughter came easily, and lasted until Kepler glanced at his watch.

"Jill, we must go," he said frantically. "Our flight leaves in ninety minutes."

"Are you kidding me? Why didn't you tell me? I would have paced the day. Are we going to make it?"

We flew to the ferry and, foregoing the horse/carriage transport, disembarked and dashed to the car. The air was chilling and the drive horrifying. Dodging other speeding cars, I noticed the dashboard indicated the convertible was traveling at 193 kilometers per hour. A mental calculation and a gasp...120 mph.

"Kep, you're getting me nervous. We're going to die driving like this. Please slow down. If we miss the flight, we'll catch one in the morning." It was obvious he was preoccupied and, despite the fact that I was shouting, heard nothing I said.

We raced against the clock and managed to get ourselves to the airport. We were out of breath and with disbelief checked the airline information board to see the flight had a two-hour delay. Hearts still pounding, the holdup was actually welcomed. In unison, we flopped into hardback seats, threw our heads back, and laughed.

"You are going to kill me, boss man. Remember I'm six years your senior. The old body is not used to jogging…and my heart can't handle your driving." I caught my breath. "That's the last time I drive *anywhere* with you."

"We'll see," he responded with an air of arrogance.

Dear friends,

I could have died in a convertible on the German auto-bahn. My heart was in my mouth and surely thought my employer had a homicide agenda. But the day was filled with awe visiting a castle and touring charming towns. The chalets dotted the hills in a storybook set-ting. There is an awful lot of play connected to this job!

# An Invite for Mike...

My significant other had been holding down the fort, walking and feeding our pup, and otherwise playing the role of my secretary back in the States. Mike retrieved my mail, photographed the important pieces, and sent them via text message. He did laundry and dinner in solo mode, and although I left a freezer full of meals, he'd of course run out and have to prepare his own. We emailed daily and spoke through a website called Viber. There was no charge for connecting, and a few times we even Skyped, giving us a chance to see each other in real time.

"Honey, the family invited you over. You can stay a couple weeks and then cruise, instead of flying back home. I investigated a transatlantic from Barcelona. It ends in Ft. Lauderdale. What do you think?" He could hear my excitement at the possibility of showing him around this glorious rock.

"Not a bad idea. That was generous of them to let me stay with you. How big is the casita again?"

"What difference does it make? We'll have a great time, and there's a pull-out couch if you think the bed is too tight," I added, feeling like I needed to convince him. "Think about it tonight and let me know in the morning." We ended the conversation with food for thought. A meal. A feast. An opportunity. Hoped he would say yes.

Less than twenty-four hours after my proposal, his transatlantic cruise was booked. He managed to be bumped from a standard room to a mini-suite, with added footage and a larger balcony. Even though initially the thought of cruising alone appeared lukewarm to him, he was now enthralled. Probably more excited than I've ever seen him, he sent email photos of the ship and side trips he could take when the ship docked in Tenerife and Barcelona.

"You have been so fabulous about me being gone, Hon. So glad you'll be coming over to reap some of the rewards and experience this piece of heaven."

"Me too," he replied. "It will be neat."

# An Unexpected Turn of Events...

It was two days after returning from the whirlwind Germany trip when I heard the familiar phrase "Permission to approach?"

"Kep, please stop asking that. Just come in." The look on his face made me question the reason he popped down while I was tutoring Andrew.

"We're just finishing up our lesson." Andrew tried to hang around to eavesdrop, but his father sent him out of the casita with just a facial expression. "What's up? You look like the cat that ate the canary." Realized that was an American idiom and clarified its meaning.

"Jill, you need to pack. We are leaving day after tomorrow," he said in a staccato voice. "We just found out information about the curriculum at Andrew's village school." He sounded disjointed, scattered. "We prefer a more academic program and have made the difficult decision to enroll our son in an American school.

I held my breath, waiting for the details that would involve me.

"We are sending you to California. Irina will pick you up at the Monterrey International Airport and introduce you to our home in Pebble Beach. Andrew and I will be arriving later that night." He paused to catch his breath. "And Jill, thank you for being so cooperative. Sometimes our life is a little crazy." He smiled a half smile, like a million plans were running through his mind.

"All righty then," I responded with an unintentional sarcastic twist. My own thoughts were exploding like discharged electrodes. Have to say good-bye to new Ibiza friends. An endless list of banal chores morphed into inappropriate laughter. "Kep, you guys are so funny. I thought I was the most spontaneous person, but you and Irina make me look like an amateur." With an obvious sigh, I melted into the wooden chair like a spineless paramecium. I shook my head in disbelief and finally asked, "How can I help you get ready?"

The cruise that Mike booked to Spain never crossed my mind.

# Novels Are Made of This...

Forty-eight hours later, my luggage and I boarded Ryanair for the first leg of a seemingly endless trek to the Golden State. The spontaneous departure carried with it both a sense of urgency and a sense of adventure. I've read novels whose main character led the life I was now leading. But they hadn't walked the planet for six decades, and certainly didn't transport themselves from a retirement recliner to intercontinental jet-setting like I did. They were characters whose author penned them long legs and snow-white teeth. They were young and beautiful, and for a moment in my mind, their sophistication was draped over my life.

I sat in the plane sincerely wondering how I got there. It was like examining your life when you were eighteen years old—you knew everything, or at least you thought you did, and suddenly you were shuffling outside your senior home to retrieve your mail forty-five years later. What happened to the time sandwiched between youth and the age to collect a Social Security check? Did it whiz by, or did it not exist in the first place?

My endless flight, broken up into three separate takeoffs and landings, kept me from swallowing something to help me sleep, and despite the drudgery of the hours in the air, I spoke to no one sitting near me. It was a nine-hour time difference from Ibiza, and obviously my circadian rhythm would be thrown off course by the time the aircraft landed. Repeatedly looked at my watch to decide when to take my blood pressure medication, the one that keeps me from losing sight in the already damaged eye.

It was not a relaxing flight. Thoughts shot about my mind triggered by constant change of plans. Sad to leave the spectacular Mediterranean island on such short notice, and although I physically departed, I felt like my soul was left behind.

I shut my eyes to revel in the fantasy. For a moment I was wearing a younger girl's clothes, a coed carrying a college ID, jetting off to meet a much older gentleman friend. The illusion evaporated with a puff of flatulence, compounded by the aroma from the spicy tacos I had inhaled at the airport. A stunning model to a gassy senior in less than 2.4 seconds.

# The Pickup to 93953…

As promised, Irina was waiting for me at the Monterrey International Airport. Gathered my luggage, and we headed to the parking lot.

"So great to see you again, Jill." We hugged, and she offered a genuine smile. "I didn't know you were coming until two days ago."

"I hope it is not a problem. Kep sprung this up on me unexpectedly. Something to do with Andrew's school on Ibiza."

"Yes, but I was expecting Kepler at the end of the year. Not so soon," she added.

"What do you have, a little pool boy stashed away?" I threw out jokingly. She returned a meek smile.

"I'm in the middle of renovations, and Kep, well, doesn't know about them." Her shoulders shrugged and we began to walk. I wondered what kind of renovations you could keep from your spouse but decided to let her disclosure drop.

"What are you driving these days?" We seemed to be moving aimlessly, her neck stretched to search down each aisle. "What am I looking for?"

"Kep bought me a Bentley. A convertible. He hasn't even seen it yet." Irina's eyes darted from one parking lane to another. "Where did I park?" She seemed scattered, anxious, not her usual in-control demeanor. "I hope I didn't get a ding in the door. These parking spaces are so close."

I stopped abruptly, hoping she would follow my lead, but she carried on. "Irina, stop! What's wrong with you? This is not the same woman I last shared wine with in Spain." My eyes searched her face for answers but found none.

"This is serious," she said. My curiosity was piqued. She continued to fret, short footsteps almost darting in multiple directions.

"*What's* serious? What the hell is going on? You are going to have a heart attack at this rate. Fess up. What's the deal?" I pursued.

When Irina left Ibiza we were friends. We shared secrets only women do and laughed at the foibles of our men. Unchilled wine in imported crystal goblets loosened our thoughts, and on more than a few occasions, we traveled together from tears to uncontrollable laughter. Discussions covered mundane issues on motherhood and more complex talks about European refugees. She admitted she was selfish and secretive, both flaws I agreed with. But Irina had another side; she sincerely wanted everyone around her to have a good time. She was gracious but not necessarily to Kep. On any given day their interaction could be filled with love or consumed with bicker. Once at main meal, their squabbling became a game, like siblings tugging at the same toy.

"Will you two stop this already? You're arguing over nothing. I honestly think you guys enjoy this, but it makes other people uncomfortable." Without finishing my meal, I excused myself from the table and wondered how little Andrew emotionally handled it. He seemed fine. I wasn't.

Irina opened up. "Well, I bought a grand piano, Steinway."

"What's wrong with that? You're a concert pianist, and Andrew plays as well. It must look terrific in the new house," I said.

"Well, we already had one. This is the second one, and it really doesn't fit anywhere." She sincerely seemed perplexed. "But it was such a good deal I couldn't pass it up." She stared me in the eye as if to seek absolution. "Kep is going to kill me. Honestly, he'll be infuriated."

"Oh, for crying out loud. After a night of passion, he'll give in," I offered.

"No way. I'm not wasting a night for a piano! I'll save that for something *big*."

She was back. Her sense of humor. Her honesty. Her outlook so different than mine. I liked her and enjoyed our time together. We laughed heartily and began the short ride to Pebble Beach to meet their new home. Although the drive was brief, there was time to mull over the new guidelines for the job I was hired to perform. Because Andrew would be attending a traditional American school, my job would be to tutor him and get him up to speed on American traditions. My first obligation was to meet the teacher.

The Bentley floated above the road. No street bumps could be detected, and the silence inside reminded me of a home with double-paned high-impact windows. I sank into the overstuffed leather seat, inhaled the sweet scent of the new high-quality hide, and tried to stay awake.

The neighborhood had a manned guard gate, and Irina offered a less-than-enthusiastic wave before we pulled through. Meandering roads on a steep climb ended at their driveway at yet another gate—iron, tall, imposing. She clicked the remote and like a queen approaching her castle drove the Bentley to the bank of garages and turned to me, using an American idiom. "This is where we hang our hat, Jill. Do you like it?"

"Oh my God, Irina. Are you kidding me?" The structure was mostly glass, floor to ceiling in configurations reminding me of stackable children's blocks. Or cargo ship containers perched in various directions on top of each other. Or a modern mansion I had no business living in. It was striking, immense, exquisite.

The trunk opened itself and Billy, the grounds man, strolled around the car with tight faded jeans and heavily broken-in cowboy boots. Despite there being a chill in the air, the man was shirtless. I could not help but notice the results of his dedication to the gym as he effortlessly lifted my luggage.

"Jill, this is Billy. This house couldn't run without him. If you need anything, our star employee here will get it for you." She brushed his bare back and smiled.

I learned later that Billy was forty-four years old. Even with his long hours, a gym workout and jogging were staples of his day. He may have looked a little "rough around the edges" but probably could fix anything and would be their gofer kind of workman.

Despite the house being mostly glass, the double front doors were wood, whitewashed with nickel handles the length of a baseball bat. The modern door knocker was made of the same metal and reflected the family initials.

Irina threw open the doors to reveal white marble flooring and original Peter Max artwork hanging on silver wires against stark white walls. I noted two Remington pieces, a traditional touch in a very futuristic home.

Two steps down led to the formal dining area, displaying a glass table that would comfortably accommodate fifteen. Ribbons of silver metal ran through the glass like knitting needles, and an immense chandelier adorned the room, sharing the same design. The lighting was more modern than I care for and later learned it came with a $19,000 price tag.

"Let me show you to your room, Jill. I hope you like it. It's at the end of the hall, so you'll have plenty of privacy."

We seemed to walk further than a residential corridor should be but finally reached the quarters I would call my own for the next few months. The room housed a queen-size bed and was surprisingly furnished in an Eastern European design; antiques from Irina's homeland she evidently had sent over to create more warmth in the modern glass-and-metal home.

Billy burst into the room. "Where do you want these, little lady?"

Irina spun in a flash. "Billy, please! This is Andrew's tutor. Please call her Jill."

"OK, Jill, little lady." He stood the three pieces of luggage neatly in the corner, flashed a wink, and left. Irreverent and confident. I immediately liked the man.

Irina began almost apologetically, "We have no chef yet. But there's fruit and some wine and cheese in the fridge. Help yourself. I have some things to do before I pick up Andrew and Kep." I noticed she placed Kep's name at the end of the sentence. "Kep's only seen this place once, but that was with the real estate agent, and he hasn't seen any of the renovations or furnishings. I'm afraid I went a little over budget." She rolled her eyes. "I hope he likes everything."

"It's out of this world. You have great taste. He'll love it." I paused. "Well, maybe the dual grand pianos may be a tad much." I laughed, but rather than a smile, my comment brought worry to her face.

She left for the airport to welcome her husband and son. I was left on four cliff side acres with a shirtless stranger I knew nothing about.

*Dear Diary,*

*I am living in a glass house. The Pacific is rolling white-caps toward the shore, but I can hear nothing. The visual is majestic. I hope I can make a difference with little Andrew and help him slip into American customs.*

Forty-five minutes later the Bentley pulled into the compound. Andrew hopped out and, having never seen his new American home, scampered around it like you'd expect a child would. "This is *big*," he declared. "Where's my room?" Kep stepped out of the Bentley.

"Do you like my wife's new car?" he asked with a strong sarcastic ingredient. He waved his hand through the air. "How about her new house?"

I thought it unusual how they interacted, and because they traveled apart so often, my observation of them being together brought new light to their relationship.

"Kep, you and Irina have a beautiful home. I know you'll be happy here."

We were all exhausted, the three of us having flown halfway around the planet. Kep used his points in business class and I used the other half of the original ticket they had bought for me on a different airline. The trip probably would have seemed faster had we traveled together, but it did not work out that way.

We grabbed a bite at the kitchen table. Each of the three special people got a hug and a smile, and then barely staying awake, I shuffled to my room.

About an hour after falling asleep, voices woke me. The squabbling had begun.

Dear friends,

Arrived safely in Pebble Beach. Gorgeous area with massive homes mostly of glass overlooking the Pacific. Took the last week to get familiar with the area. Expensive everything. Student and I to movies at double the price of Florida fares.

House is stacked like shipping containers. Music is piped through all the areas and fresh flowers sit on each table and in all bathrooms. We have champagne nightly and open crates that arrive daily with international artifacts.

No billboards permitted in the town, and finding a store requires multiple rides past it.

In heaven...very different from Ibiza but still a slice of Shangri-la.

*Dear Diary,*

*For the first time I'm wondering if I made the right decision continuing with this job. It's perfect in every way, but there's a vibe that is disconcerting, and I can't put my finger on it. Maybe it's rattling around this enormous home, maybe it's determining what my job will actually be. Somehow I can't justify how well I'm treated just for tutoring a couple hours a day. Maybe time will make my position more clear. Maybe not.*

# Grab Your Hat, Sugarplum, We're on the Road Again...

Twenty days after arriving in Pebble Beach, Kep left for another of their properties, this one on a remote island near Hawaii.

"When do you think you'll be back?" I asked, although it was none of my business.

"Not sure. If you need anything, or if Andrew misbehaves, email me."

I knew there would be no communication, as I needed absolutely nothing and Andrew *never* misbehaved.

The routine of Andrew's school time, tutoring, and accompanying Irina on various shopping jaunts was becoming comfortable. But as I learned in Ibiza, change is part of the plan. A shift in itinerary or agenda was the rule rather than the exception, and the only thing that was constant with this job was...change!

"Jill, we will be leaving in two hours. Can you be ready?" It was rhetorical. Of course I'd be ready.

"Where are we headed?" I asked as if it mattered. "How long will we be gone? What sort of clothes do I need to pack?"

Pouring espresso and only half paying attention to my questions, Irina responded. "We are going up to San Francisco for a few nights."

If a week meant a month, I wondered how long "a few nights" really meant.

"We will be staying at my sister's house. As you know Andrew has no school Monday, so we'll be back by Tuesday morning. Please bring materials to tutor him over the weekend."

Dear friends,

I used to look like Princess Di. Now I look like Camilla.

*Dear Diary,*

*I'm off again, this time to San Francisco. Not sure how long I can keep up this pace. Really enjoying the opportunities this fabulous job offers. Andrew is a doll, and his lessons are going well. Still not homesick.*

Several days spent with Irina's sister and her family. Lovely, gracious, all-around pleasant visit. Andrew and I worked on a desk in the living room and then toured locally. The trip home, amidst heavy traffic, lulled my little man to sleep in the backseat. The extra hours in the bumper-to-bumper line of cars gave my employer and me time to enjoy girl talk. It was no-holds-barred:

past loves, college escapades, first jobs. We laughed and reconnected like during the fun times we had on Ibiza, although Irina was rarely there more than a couple weeks at a time. It was a stutter lifestyle, not fluid, not predictable.

Dear friends,

Ready to inhale chamomile; no, maybe take it in an IV drip. Need to stay in one place long enough for the tea to actually brew, but won't happen when living with a family full of vitality and the wherewithal to act on a whim.

Tried sprucing up this tired face. Learned something simplistic: don't shave off your eyebrow when you live on an estate. Wealthy folks are gracious and won't mention the fact that the hired tutor teaches with a solo-brow. Penciling it in is an act of futility, especially if the pencil is black and the other brow is gray.

How does part two of this position compare to part one in Spain? Well, we all speak English, I can navigate using a GPS, and I share the grocery store aisles with other folks who have digested a box or two of Cracker Jack. Some skinnies, but not nearly the number that strolled the beaches of Ibiza. Am I homesick? Not even close.

# A Collection of Service Workers...

Electrician, plumber, designer, and gardener joined the parade of other workers on the estate. Billy, the grounds man, was trusted by the family and, despite his being shirtless most of the time, was in charge. His vocabulary appeared to blossom from a previous visit to some form of incarceration, and the use of the *F* word was commonplace. He drove a red pickup truck with the word STUD in large gold italics across the door on the passenger side. On one occasion I overheard Irina making a plea to Kep to have the truck repainted. As of this writing, it's still red...and still has STUD plastered across the door. And still turns heads in the exclusive Pebble Beach neighborhood.

For some reason, Billy took a liking to me. Maybe my "mature" appearance reminded him of his mother; maybe he simply felt the positive vibe and quiet chuckle he brought my way. Many times, Billy would stop by my room to run one problem or another by me for solutions. Other times it was advice for the lovelorn, which I found hard to believe given his charisma and magazine-cover physique. With muddy cowboy boots and equally grungy dungarees, he'd flop down on my bed, disregarding the fact that the designer comforter probably cost the mortgage payment of the average American. The word *cooties* crossed my mind more than once. Being a counselor was not in my job description, but my religious conviction believed wise words were channeled through God. If I could play the role of the voice of reason, I'd do it cheerfully.

# New Digs for the Tutor...

A bout a hundred feet from the main house, very much like the setup on Ibiza, was a pavilion with partial kitchen (no stove), full bathroom, and sauna. Modern cabinetry housed a Murphy bed, queen size, and upon pulling it down initially, I found mouse droppings on the mattress cover. No other sign of damage; in fact, it looked like it had never been used. Two comfortable chairs occupied the corners. An antique table the size of a hula hoop, with two matching cane-and-wood high-back chairs completed the decor. Granite ran ten feet against a far wall, under which was a refrigerator and cupboards full of appliances: microwave, portable stovetop, blender, etc. There were dishes and cups, baking utensils and condiments. Forks, knives, and spoons, however, were AWOL. Not one to be found.

Some folks are resourceful. I'm not one of them. But I do keep stuff in my handbag in case Aborigines take over the world or other equally plausible earthly catastrophes occur.

The one spork I excavated from the bottom of my Dooney & Bourke was still sealed in cellophane, acceptable to even the most highly acclaimed germophobe.

I used it for a full week, forgetting on each shopping excursion to pick up more.

"Irina, the pavilion is adorable. I'd like to move over there," I mentioned after discovering the sweet retreat. "It will give you more privacy and be good for me as well."

"Oh *no*, Jill. You'll be more comfortable in the main house. You can hang out there after you wake up, if you like. You can even shower and have breakfast there. But we'd like you to sleep here." It was not debated. It was not an option. The end of discussion.

Irina actually made the right call. The nights where Andrew's both parents were out of town, he slept in the guest room next to mine, assuring us both emotional security while we rambled around the eight-thousand-square-foot home.

Pebble Beach gets cold. Unlike the dependable warmth of Florida, sleeping in a sweat suit became the rule rather than the exception.

Each morning, with fresh clothes in tow, I'd scoot down the path to the pavilion. A warm shower, cup of Earl Grey, and bowl of oatmeal inspired the daily scurry. Morning routine completed, I'd pop over to the main house to check out the day's agenda.

Kep and Irina woke up more in love than when the previous night fell. Somehow the result of an overnight metamorphic transformation. Bickering the previous evening, the dawn presented the couple with smiles and easy chatter. It was like a game, routine display of unusual behavior.

# The Tutor Runs on High Test...

M aybe it was caffeine, maybe just the fact that I was enormously fulfilled, my job hit high gear. Made calls to register Andrew for Cub Scouts, locating a convenient meeting place and time and trekked clear across the mountain to the only Scout uniform shop to gear him up. Picked up the shirt and patches and made haste back home to hand-sew the six emblems in the exact position Boy Scouts of America mandates. Thimble-less fingertips pierced multiple times by the needle, I wondered why the tutor would be taking on this responsibility. Andrew was special, and I wanted him to fit in with American children, that's why!

Hung the navy blue shirt on a hanger to admire my seamstress skills. Awful. Terrible. Absolutely not acceptable. The only option was to find a professional and ask him/her to have it done by the next day and soothe my ego.

An Asian woman a zillion years old sat hunched over an old sewing machine in nearby Monterrey. In broken English we communicated enough for her to understand the importance of having this job completed ASAP.

"You come back in one week." She seemed to struggle with the language.

"Ma'am, it really needs to be done by tomorrow. It's *very* important." I continued, almost begging. "Maybe you just need something to give you energy. I noticed there is a French bakery across the street. Do you think a little pastry and coffee could energize you?"

"Nothing with cheese," she responded, surprisingly in almost perfect English.

I bolted out of the shop and dashed across the street. The aroma of fresh-out-of-the-oven delights tempted me, but time was of the essence. Grabbing her coffee and flaky apple turnover, I ran back across to the shop. By the time I offered her the wrapped pastry, the shirt patches were attached. Neatly. Somehow I felt like I cheated and should slip into the car incognito with trench coat and sunglasses. But the deed was done and my star student would have a Cub Scouts uniform just like the other kids. I realized there was very little I wouldn't do for this child. Andrew touched my heart with his sweet disposition.

It was obvious teaching was only one component of this unique job. Somewhere along the way, it morphed into being a governess and personal assistant to Irina.

"Irina, Andrew has no spiritual background. Why don't we get him into religion classes and have him make his First Communion?"

"Jill, *yes*! Thank you so much. Could you do the leg-work and find out where he needs to be?" She grabbed her keys and headed to the garage. "Let me know if you need any money."

In a flash, I had another project. Grabbed my cell phone, found the name of the local church, and began the process.

Dear friends,

Sun, fog, clouds, sun, fog, clouds…repeat endlessly. It's the weather pattern on the West Coast.

Well driller, water filter installer, house cleaner… the parade of folks who make a house a home. A lot of orchestration, but Irina excels at that and has it running like a well-oiled machine.

Offered to clean up the kitchen. Swept place mats off the table and rinsed them under the faucet. The lady of the house gasped: they were leather, imported from Italy. Yikes.

Registered my student for Cub Scouts and religion class. The grounds man declared all Boy Scouts are "faggots." My student asked me what a faggot was. I told him it meant a kid who likes to go camping.

My little man is well on his way to being a typical American boy who likes bugs and *Star Wars*, only he's trilingual and has been to twenty-four countries. I think I need to write a book.

# Mr. Max...

T he full moon aggravated my sleep, and with acti-
vated dream states, the night could be categorized
as disastrous. A knock on my bedroom door:

"Jill, can I come in?" It was Andrew.

"Sure, Bubba. You're up early."

"We want to say 'Good morning' to you," he
said sweetly.

"Who's *we*?" I inquired.

In slithered my student and his pal Max, a ball
python journeying around his neck like it was a perfectly normal greeting.

"*Are you kidding me? Get out! Now!*" I shouted. "If
you bring that reptile in here again, I'll cut him in half
and you'll leave with *two* snakes."

"Jill, you need to bond with him. I promise you'll
learn to like him."

"Turn around and keep walking," I commanded.
"And don't stop until you hit San Diego."

As he left my room, I heard him say something to
the effect of, "She's usually a lot nicer. Just a bad first
impression." Who the heck was he talking to?

And that's how I met the newest member of
the family.

Snakes eat mice, generally live ones, but Max liked "pinkies." Those were newborn mice, frozen and sold in packs of two. They had to be defrosted, or as I later learned after Irina actually did it, placed on a napkin in the microwave and dropped into the cage. The entire process was revolting. And repeated every other week.

Andrew meandered into the dedicated room of the house used for tutoring. His hands were empty, but peeking out of the top of his shirt was a darting tongue and beady eyes gleaming with malice.

"Oh my God. Seriously?" I could feel my blood pressure rising. "Do *not*, I repeat, do *not* come to class with that serpent. That was not in the job description!"

With his usual quick-witted retort, he said, "You didn't read page *two*."

Max was not carried. He was worn. Sometimes Andrew had him snuggled in his shirtsleeve, other times around his neck like jewelry.

Irina was perfectly fine with the snake, and because Kep was still out of town, he had not had the pleasure of meeting his son's new acquisition.

Puppies are cute. Even little porcupines can be enchanting. Snakes, however, have no redeeming qualities, and this tutor made it abundantly clear how she felt. Unfortunately, before this manuscript went to publication, Mr. Max went to heaven.

# The Counselor Hangs Her Shingle...

As in Ibiza, relatives would visit the family for extended periods of time. They appeared to pop in without warning and left with spontaneous departure. A carousel lifestyle that somehow incorporated me and what they conceived as my words of wisdom. Not sure if it was my bluntly honest interpretation of their "issues" or the fact that my responses represented a generation or two before their birth.

Billy was a regular "client." Any hour, any day could see the stage set.

"Hey, little lady. Got a minute?" He was already inside the pavilion, not awaiting a response. We'd grab the sage-plaid overstuffed chairs and begin our "talks." Each lasted just under an hour, with his departure encouraging a calmer day for this kind-hearted albeit unusual character.

One day, without exaggeration or embellishment for the benefit of this book, the "stream" of family kept me chatting from breakfast time right through noon. My little pavilion was no-cost therapy for those who preferred advice from an older, less gracious (more honest) individual.

Billy was just finishing up when Irina opened the pavilion door, popped her head in, and told him to get back to work.

"Jill, do you have a minute?" Without an answer, she began. "What is your take on...?" Because the woman is bright, the talk was not a lecture or plea to agree with her version of whatever issue carried her to get another opinion in the first place. In an abbreviated capsule, information was dispelled by her, digested by me, and regurgitated into what advice this outsider could offer. Our "sessions" always ended in Irina reaching to embrace me, thanking me for my forthright words, and an invite to champagne that evening. We all shared the bubbly every night anyway, so the invitation was simply just a reflection of the wealthy having a tremendously gracious demeanor.

"Permission to approach?" It was Kep calling out while I tried to pop into the bathroom.

"Come in, Kep. I'll be right out." Sort of embarrassing having your boss hear the toilet flush, but with a string of "visitors" that morning, it was unavoidable. "What can I get you? Tea, coffee?"

"Nothing. Am I interfering? Do you have a minute?" A "minute" was always thirty or more. We each grabbed a chair. He began our talks with humor. Wit, sarcasm, the rhetoric that would take him as a native of the metro tri-state area; New York, New Jersey, Connecticut.

Initially the exchange of dialogue was dominated by him, either because he was used to that in his world of business, or maybe to show he was the boss. Not sure the reason, but within minutes, the podium reversed, and I was the one in control of the gavel.

"I have a business opportunity. Wondered what you think," he began one day. Never really understood why such a successful man would care what a retired schoolteacher would think, but I listened and learned volumes. Most of the businesses were in Asia and Europe, requiring Kep to be away more time than he was at home. Irina was always offered to join him, but during the eight months I lived with the family, she never once took that option.

The pavilion door popped open with a simultaneous knock. A family member, already on the compound more than two weeks, asked if I had a second to talk. "Kep, I didn't see you there. Are you almost finished?' She *had* seen him, made the conscious decision to interrupt, and without remorse waited for Kep's chair to be vacated like a restaurant table with an impatient diner.

The scenario was repeated at least twice weekly and each time became the impetus of conversations with the good Lord. Asked for guidance to give sound advice so other lives could be more productive and happier.

*Dear Diary,*

*I have no formal training to offer in the counseling arena. Wondering why people assume I do. Hoping lives are improved not made more challenging by my words. Maybe folks know their stories are under lock and key. I could keep a secret. I could offer brutally honest opinions without being judgmental. Guess that's why!*

Dear Friends,

Feel like a psychologist without training. So many approaches to get "my take" on everything from decorating to business ventures. Some lovelorn discussions and various complaints about one thing or another. If I had to list the parameters of this job, it would sound like processed fabrication. Not complaining, just appreciative of how much I'm learning.

This job makes me feel special.

# Trying to Be "Normal"

Playing the role of governess and personal assistant, my cell phone number was the "go-to" means of communication. All trivial matters could be taken care of without bothering Irina and having the benefit of multitasking ability; I could organize the family's day and make sure Andrew did what he was supposed to.

Met with the teacher on a regular basis, attended parties in class, and tutored my little guy. It was time to move to meeting other parents and inviting some boys over to play. Only *they* probably didn't live in a home that required an intercom system and a bank of garages on a multi-acre estate. Perched on a steep cliff. Overlooking the Pacific. I could bet on that.

One afternoon, outside Andrew's classroom, I met a young mother whose boy had befriended my student. We exchanged numbers and made arrangements for the children to play Friday afternoon.

A phone call: "Hi Jill. This is Jessica, Cole's mom. I was thinking Andrew could come over right after school this Friday. I'll pick him up when I pick up Cole." The mere thought of me sending my charge to a stranger's house was unimaginable.

"Hey, Jessica. I'm glad you called. Andrew would love to play at your place. But being old comes with being old-fashioned, so I really need to see your house and meet the family first. Would you mind terribly? I know it sounds silly." I felt like I had to defend myself. A quick twist in approach, I continued, "Andrew's parents are very strict and I'm just doing my job."

That Friday, with Andrew in the front seat, we put the address into the GPS. Down a winding road, gravel, lined by bungalows displaying axle-less roadsters, broken porch doors, and various missing window shutters replaced with mismatched substitutes, we succeeded in locating the address. His school buddy ran out to greet us.

"Oh my God, Andrew. I don't know about this," I whispered, extremely concerned.

"Jill, it's fine. They even have an old school bus we can play in." At nine years old, he knew this place was *not* fine. Jessica welcomed us. She looked clean enough, but I needed to see the inside of the house.

"Jessica, I know this is weird, but would you mind if I came inside for a minute just to put my mind at ease?"

She complied with a smile, never acknowledging the various automobiles strewn about her property that appeared to have died a fiery death decades ago.

The house was clean despite having four young children and a cat. It was decision time, and in a split second I said I'd go for coffee up the hill and pick him up in an hour. I explained that Andrew had something else on his schedule so today's playdate would be abbreviated. How much can kids run through abandoned buses anyway? God help me.

By the grace of God, my little Andrew survived playing on "the other side of the tracks." As an afterthought, he probably learned how lucky he was having help around his house and grateful he was so well traveled. Or maybe he was just a nine-year-old boy pretend playing like kids do.

"Jessica, thank you so much. Why don't you bring Cole over next Friday, and the boys can play again?" There was no mention of the full-size theater or trampoline. Never brought up the fact that Andrew's mom would be enjoying the week at a Northern California spa and I would be in charge. Wondering if romping through an old school bus would trump a media center lined with leather recliners. Even with the popcorn I'd make them, kids living on the planet for less than a decade prefer the empty box over the gift and a broken-down vehicle over a movie. I had seven days to worry about this.

The neighborhood gate guard called the house announcing Cole and his mother. The drive from the subdivision entrance to the private second gate on the property was about a minute. I ran to the lower private gate leading onto the estate to let her in, hopped into her front seat, and although I offered her a smile, we exchanged absolutely no dialogue. About twenty-nine seconds of silence passed as she steered her car to the base of the imposing residence. Awkward. Solemn. She looked terrified.

We finally made small talk as we entered the front doors, and it was at that moment it became abundantly clear Andrew's life was *not* like other children his age, and denial on my part did not erase the facts. No other boys came to play at Andrew's house again.

Dear friends,

My student had a friend over. The child was fine, but the mother was intimidated by the imposing residence. Just like I was when I first set eyes on it. Helping my student make friends will take some work.

Getting more comfortable in California. It was time for a pedicure, and made the attempt yesterday. Called to be sure the cost didn't equal a mortgage payment. Always bring my own polish, so stopped into CVS to pick some up. The least expensive, although it was a no-name brand, was none dollars. Seriously? Off to another store, more on a boutique scale, and the price was almost double. The idea of sharing polish with strangers all using the same pedicure shop was atrocious. Sauntered into salon and lifted a minimum of eight bottles, looking for one that was new, one no one would ever choose. Found it! Somewhere between plum and the color of chewed gum scraped off the sole of a wingtip shoe. Brand spanking new.

Worst pedicure ever. Polish all over toes, sloppy.

Searching for inertia. Not to be found at this employment.

Irina purchased a board game for fifty-five dollars. Pretty sure my own children had that game and entirely positive it cost less than twelve dollars. Engaged Andrew playing on the game room table. More busy-ness.

*Dear Diary,*

*School pictures were scheduled for mid-October. Mentioned it to Irina, but she will forget. I'll be sure to have him spiffed up.*

*Have to remember to get Andrew his own library card tomorrow after school.*

*If my role was undefined previously, it's now as clear as a newly washed window. A "Jill of all trades," and I wouldn't change it for a night on the town with Ryan Gosling. Well, OK, maybe for that.*

# What Is It *Really* Like?

There is an emotional component when you are trusted and integrated into another family's life. You feel obligated not to let them down, to work with extra fervor, to earn your keep. Because they are so gracious, it's easy to put in extra hours.

A friend from home asked if jealousy played a role. Incredibly, it doesn't, and while I'm benefitting from a life of wealth, it's not *my* life. I feel lucky to have experienced it, but I realize the situation is temporary. Materialism has never been part of my personality, but having services to make life 'more gentle' certainly is. A masseuse, laundress, and chef could easily be something to scribble on my wish list for Santa.

Wealth is a mind-set proving the world is an easy place to navigate. Having said that, lottery tickets will be regularly purchased when I get back home.

Kep is out of the country. When he left, the silliness, impetuous outings, and chocolate bars slowed to a halt. Madcap antics he entertained me with are sorely missed, and now donning a cap of seriousness is something I need to get used to. The family is the same, the job has changed: it morphed into a determination to get

Irina organized and make Andrew entirely comfortable living in America.

In Ibiza, the tutor's job came with help. The "help" had help of her own. In California, I *am* the help, another pair of hands to move boxes or house-sit until a delivery arrives. I'm the one who calls the repairman, who gets a copy of a key made, who picks up a prescription from the pharmacy. My job is to line up play-dates and prepare Andrew for Cub Scouts meetings. I accompany him to church on Sundays and take him to religion class afterward. In layman's terms, I'm the live-in grandma integrating an education faction.

Which job do I like the most? Both. Teaching daily and being treated like a quasi-princess in Spain was spectacular. But working more hours with varied responsibilities is also rewarding. Doing my job in English eliminates frustration, but the charm of Europe is missing. I enjoyed studying the interesting differences in culture, but to some extent the folks hanging their hat in Pebble Beach, California, have a culture of their own as well.

Whole Foods in the Del Monte Shopping Center was the go-to grocery store the family preferred. Grabbed a chair and sipped a decaf, digesting traits of humanity the wealthy demonstrate. In an hour I observed the following:

Older gent in almost-florescent green golf pants, pink-and-green collared shirt, pocketless, with a full head of white hair. Down south were saddle shoes, suede, but up north was an index finger resting comfortably in his nostril. He appeared to be excavating whatever evidence of life inhabited his nasal cavity.

Another man stopped to readjust his personal pride. One hand on his zipper, the other on the grocery cart, he shifted one leg like a pup on a fire hydrant. A shake of his hindquarters appeared to help in the readjustment. He was either well-endowed or had a prosthetic gone bad.

A young Caucasian mother displaying tanned, muscular legs framed on the top by her tennis whites strolled to the coffee counter. She was accompanied by an African American gal in a uniform-like outfit displaying PACIFIC SUNSET embroidered on her cotton blouse. In the cart was a blond-haired toddler, too old to inhale the pacifier that occupied the entire real estate of her mouth. I pulled out my iPhone to ask Siri if Pacific Sunset was the name of a golf course or simply a private residence. It was *not* the name of a business establishment. A young mom treading through life with a nanny was indeed a study in culture.

Hopped into the Honda I paid $1,800 to transport across the country and headed back to my fantasy life.

# The School...

T here were three options for schooling: Stevenson, with a $25,600 price tag; Monterrey Bay Charter School, with random admission lottery drawings; or the local public school. Andrew's parents enrolled their son in the paperless, computer-driven, rated number ten public school.

Homework nightly, and although I spent twenty-nine years in the classroom, I've not seen assignments like he had.

"What is the philosophical differences in the hierarchy..." Essentially what the teacher wanted was to compare how the author of the book she assigned felt internally as opposed to how students felt while reading it. Say what? The children are in grade four. Every night homework took a minimum of one and a half hours. That was *before* tutoring.

Each pupil was issued a laptop and whiteboard. Classroom work was generated from online sources, and the five adults in *each* classroom were ready to offer assistance if needed. Three of the adults were on the payroll; the others were daily volunteers. In New York, where I taught, parents/volunteers were prohibited from infringing on classroom lessons. We had a strong union, and that contributed to mandating a single instructor be in each classroom.

A call from the teacher requested me to help with the Halloween party.

"Hi, Jill. It's Emma Brooks, Andrew's teacher. I was wondering if you could help out at the Halloween party." She paused. "Would you mind bringing carrots?" I asked her to repeat herself. "Carrots. If you could bring them, that would be great. We have celery and hummus already. One mom is making veggie dip. That will be special."

Special? Where are the cupcakes and candy corn? Where's the sugar, Buttercup?

"Sure, I'll bring the carrots. Anything else?"

"Well, if you want to buy a large bottle of V-8, it would be appreciated."

I looked at the phone and wondered if this was a joke. Typed a memo on my cell: "Bring carrots and V-8 to school." Never typed the word "party."

Spent an hour at Andrew's school. Room set up with "treats" such as grapes, strawberries, and string cheese. Oh yes, there were carrots, and of course a yummy way to wash it all down: V-8.

Kids' costumes were original. No store-bought, run-of-the-mill garb you could pick up at Target for less than ten dollars. There were scarecrows and Ninja warriors, a cat and a nurse. It was apparent the mothers (or their nannies) took time to create authentic attire, which continued the theme of "all natural." For a state or this specific town, with so many beautiful people (helped by cosmetic nips and tucks), I found it sort of ironic that the "natural" philosophy did not carry over to personal appearance. Cosmetic surgeons inhabited seven pages of the phone book.

Halloween night, we took Andrew to a more child-friendly town. Kep FaceTimed to be part of his son's night, despite it being three a.m. where he was. He watched his boy ring doorbells and collect goodies, sharing in the excitement with his only child. My heart sank when I focused on Kep's eyes. He was clear across the planet during such an important milestone, and although it was none of my business, I couldn't help but wonder why his international work could not have waited until Halloween passed. I thanked Kep for making the effort to touch base and handed the phone to his wife.

"Kep, we're in the middle of trick-or-treating. Call tomorrow." The phone was silenced and handed back to me right in the middle of his reply.

# The Tutor Turns Headhunter...

"Jill, we need a chef. Could you see about advertising online?" Irina stopped to capture her thoughts. "We prefer someone who speaks Spanish so Andrew doesn't forget the language."

"Sure," I replied, as usual. "Give me some guidelines. Salary? Hours? Duties?"

We ironed out the details and I placed a local ad. My cell rang at least fifteen times in the next few hours, forcing me to silence the ringer and simply take messages. Rosita, Maria, Luisa, and an American who spoke no Spanish and was never employed to cook stepped up to the soapbox to let me know why they were the perfect applicants.

"Adison, I'm sorry. You have no experience and my employer prefers someone who has worked in a family setting."

"I cooked for my college roommates. We had to use a hot plate, but spaghetti and soup came out perfectly," she offered seriously.

There was one gal I would have hired in a second. Interviewed her untraditionally.

"Do you like *very* big dogs?" I asked her.

"I guess so. Do they have a *big* dog?" she stammered meekly.

"No, just wanted to know if you like big dogs." I laughed, and she joined in. Immediate compatibility. Good fit. Sense of humor mandated at this household. Unfortunately, she landed another position closer to her home. The search continued.

The interviews proceeded, and some required me to drive thirty minutes to a halfway point. Some applicants never showed up, others changed their story between the time I interviewed them and when they met Irina. One said she lived alone. Her children were grown and she spoke Spanish. By week's end, we learned two teenage children lived with her, the older one fresh out of prison. Her Spanish experience was the one year she took in high school.

There was something ironic about "the help" hiring other "help." By the time I left at Thanksgiving, an appropriate chef still had not been found.

Dear friends,

My employers asked me to hire a chef. Finding help requires patience and a lie detector. More applicants than missed bull's-eyes at a dart competition. Still no one hired. The parameters of my job expand. Flexibility is the key that opens every component of this kind of work. Loving it…with a capital *L*. Wish I was twenty years younger.

# Life...

One night the family was expecting company and planned a large dinner, but I bailed to grab a bite solo. Found my position in the parade of cars at the Monterrey McDonald's drive-through. With the Honda settled in a parking spot, a "nutritious" meal of 13,500 calories could be readily inhaled. No skinny people to judge my very obvious vice. For a brief moment, a vision of Dr. Phil flew by. I think he was wagging his finger.

Mayo dripped from the unwrapped Filet-O-Fish onto my slacks, and the leaking chocolate milk container felt obligated to join in the mess.

I sat in the darkened car alone but not lonely. "I hate being fat," I whispered to no one. Stopped for Oreos on the way home, and despite being educated by Catholic school nuns, no guilt tapped me on the shoulder. I was enormously content.

Andrew was getting ready for school one morning when his alter-adult sprang into action. Being as creative and insightful as he was made teaching him pure pleasure. There was always that statement he innocently made that induced guttural guffaws. His sense of humor, obviously inherited from his father, will open doors for him…if his charm and good looks fail. Which they won't.

"I miss Bonita making us breakfast. Now my mother just slaps a cold waffle in my hand as I run out the door."

Sometimes kids say it just like they see it. No filter, just the facts. Like a witness on a courtroom stand.

Andrew has always had people who washed his clothes, cooked his favorite meals — including daily dessert — and picked up his toys. But Spain, Germany, and all his other homes are now part of his memory bank. He's simply a nine-year-old proving his mettle is strong enough to navigate the American world.

Dear friends,

Parents say I'm part of the family and will be sorely missed. This little trio is worthy of a sitcom — sweet and unpredictable. I wish they lived closer to my house. Of course, we'd never be living in the same neighborhood. Darn.

# Global Proof...

My student and his family are "global." That term defies definition, but some examples will pen the scene.

Picked up Andrew from school. For no obvious reason my fourth grader belted out "Three Blind Mice," the first part in English and the second in German. He didn't know he was doing it. When he sang it the second time, it was all in Spanish. For some reason that not only impressed me but fertilized understanding of how a multinational person engineers his thought processes.

One day Andrew dashed through the kitchen door waving a book order form he was given in class. He had never seen one of them and was enormously excited.

"Jill, can I order *Diary of a Wimpy Kid*?"

"Absolutely, my little man. Mom will be pleased you are reading."

"But Jill. Should I order it in Spanish or English?" An innocent question with no hidden implications.

"At least you didn't ask if you should order it in German," I chuckled.

"It doesn't come in German," was his factual reply.

Because Kep traveled so often, Irina and her son dined out on a regular basis. Of course they invited me, the "help," for no reason other than they would have another person with whom to chat. Restaurants are not fast food but rather elegant establishments where one must dress the part. Even Andrew slipped into long pants and got his hair combed.

Over filet mignon that Irina insisted on ordering me, the following conversation occurred verbatim:

Mom: "Wondering where we should spend Christmas this year."

Andrew: "Chicago. Not Austria again, Mommy. And not Warsaw. *Please*, Mommy!"

Mom: "We'll see. Do you want to go back to Iceland?"

Andrew: I want to see snow. And *please* not Maui. Why can't we go back to Thailand? Wait, they don't have snow there, right, Mommy? We can visit Auntie in Chicago, maybe."

The Christmas dilemma apparently surfaced annually right before Thanksgiving. Suggestions from Andrew were residences not hotels. When he told stories of visits to the Seychelles, I shook my head, for he has no idea he was in a unique situation. The family never flaunted wealth, never bragged, and donated generously to orphanages and other institutions.

"Jill, what are your plans for Christmas?" inquired Irina.

Andrew chimed in, parroting his mother. "Yeah, what *are* you doing for Christmas? We can call you and tell you where we are. Would you be able to come?"

"You guys are too sweet. My family will be visiting with the grandchildren. It's sort of a tradition. But thank you *so* much for thinking of me," I replied.

Andrew continued, "We will call you anyway, in case the family all got sick and couldn't come." I reached over to my little man with an embrace that let him know how special he was.

They wound up in Lake Tahoe, not in a residence but a five-star resort. Maybe someday I'll take them up on their invite.

# Handsome but a Character
# Nonetheless…

B illy, the groundskeeper, was somehow born sans a governor between his mind and tongue. No roadblock. No stop sign. First impression of anyone crossing his path would leave no doubt how Billy felt.

One day Mr. Graham, the president of the Pebble Beach Homeowners Association, stopped by. He introduced himself, including his position in the community. Bedecked in starched khaki slacks, golf shirt, and cordovan penny loafers, he looked like he'd been lifted off a *GQ* publication. Billy was working, which that particular day meant kneeling in pine bark mulch. He threw a glance at the gentleman and greeted him. "Hey, pops. What can I do for you?"

"The committee wishes to invite the Jankovics to a cocktail party in their honor as new residents," he began. "I wonder if you could tell me where I could find them."

"No can do, Bubaloo. But I'll be sure they get the message. Leave your card." He pointed and added, "Over there on the wheelbarrow."

In a small enclave like Pebble Beach, word gets out fast. Business cards and advertisements began pouring into the family's mailbox with suggested names of appropriate help.

Waiting on a bench outside Andrew's classroom one afternoon, I noticed Billy's familiar walk...almost a strut. Dirty jeans, flannel shirt unbuttoned from his collar to oversized belt buckle; he approached me like he was the headmaster.

"Hey, little lady. I thought I'd save you the trip of picking up Andrew. Didn't think you'd be here so early."

"Billy," I began, "you really should button up on school property. Irina would *not* be comfortable with you dressed like that.

The bell rang and the exodus of children drew the groundskeeper into the flurry. Andrew promptly spotted me and witnessed Billy moving toward the female teachers who were supervising the students, many of them taking note with obvious admiration. I grabbed my charge and almost jogged to the car. The cackle of young, giggling teachers could be heard until we reached the parking lot.

Billy had a tender heart, tremendous zest for life, and borderless parameters on appropriate behavior. His cowboy hat partnered well with his red pickup truck, but not so much with the Bentleys of Pebble Beach or the Mercedes of Monterrey. Through Billy's personal vista, there was no such thing as a bad day.

Stories/rumors flew through the Pebble Beach grapevine like greyhounds out of the racing gate. Not sure anyone checked the validity, but loud and clear was the anecdote of Billy "crashing" the Ladies' Luncheon. He apparently leaned back on a dining chair, rocking so intently that one of the wooden legs gave way, sending his own hat into projectile mode and taking with it a bowl of chowder.

Despite not being the typical employee of zip code 93953, his job was not in jeopardy. The family trusted him, not necessarily his judgment. For a family of wealth, trust reigns first. When I left California, Billy was still employed.

# A Mousetrap, Tiara, and Thanksgiving...

On days that Irina awoke well rested, often fighting sleepless nights, she was comical and silly. One morning, wearing a Victoria's Secret black nightie, covered loosely with an opened satin robe, she descended the spiral staircase donning an enormous diamond-studded tiara. She waved her hand through the air like the British queen celebrating her coronation. The reverie was broken abruptly when the buzzer sounded on the electric mousetrap under the kitchen cabinet. With one hand holding the tiara in place, the other swept across the floor, dislodging the trap.

"Got you, you little bugger," she declared to a dead mouse. Still holding the tiara in place, she managed to pull off a piece of paper towel, grab the rodent, and toss it into the garbage compactor. I stood in awe, staring at her ridiculous antics. Laughing together until tears filled my eyes, I watched her head up the staircase with the grace with which she descended ten minutes earlier, bidding adieu to the imaginary commoners who occupied her kingdom.

Some days were girlfriend-colored. We sat and shared life's secrets, like two seventh graders meeting at the coat closet in the back of their classroom. Those days were precious but appeared randomly. They hid between days of anxiety attacks and endless shopping.

Irina truly was a special woman, and I could see why Kep was so enamored by her charm. Also obvious were the demons that stole her contentment despite the storybook life she was bestowed.

The retina problem that haunted me months earlier returned, forcing my investigation into locating a specialist in California. With trepidation, I drove to the facility, was examined, and received an injection directly in the eye. Incredibly, there was no pain. The numbing spray did the job but unfortunately left me looking through a lace curtain. It did clear up eventually, but the experience was frightening. I was told my retinal vein occlusion would be an ongoing challenge requiring monthly shots. Each injection was $2,600. Luckily Good Days, a grant for folks in my category, picked up much of the cost. Thanksgiving was a week away, and certainly I would be thankful for my sight.

Early one morning, Irina slipped into my bedroom, pushed aside the comforter on the empty side of the queen-size bed, and plopped down. Still in horizontal mode, I turned my head toward her.

"Good morning. Are we having a pajama party?" Read her face and searched for a smile. There was none. "What's up, Irina? Are you OK?"

With an initial stammer, she began, "Jill, I know you are going to be with us until the end of the year. You promised. And we want you." She paused.

Trying to help her out. "But?"

"Well," she hung her head, "we will be having seventeen for Thanksgiving dinner. They will be flying in at the same time."

"They are staying over, and you need my room, right?" My guess was accurate.

"Oh Jill, yes. But I have an idea. We'll fly you home to be with your family, and you could come back the Monday after Thanksgiving. Would you be all right with that?"

I sat up in bed, reached for this sweet princess, and hugged the fit body that housed a delicate soul. "Let me think how we could make this work."

"Great. I'll go get us some coffee and we can sip it in bed." She left a smile and headed for the kitchen.

Sipping morning joe in bed with my employer would be too weird, so I hopped up, hit the bathroom, and met her at the espresso bar in the thirty-foot kitchen that overlooked the Pacific. When the conversation finished up, I decided in fact I would fly home, and just stay there. Before my departure, I'd find her another tutor and continue to work on hiring an appropriate chef for the household. Andrew and I would continue our two-hour daily lessons until I orchestrated a path to drop the news of my departure to my little man.

And then there was informing Kep, who would be flying home the day before Thanksgiving. "He is not going to take too well to this change," I whispered to myself. Called Mike to let him know his lady would be returning home a month earlier than expected.

As was usually the case, working for the family spun my head in multiple directions. While a plan alteration never affected my personality, it did wreak havoc on my digestive system.

*Dear Diary,*

*How can I ever leave this family? They have captured both my heart and soul.*

# Rumors Are Like Wildfires...

R umors spread like wildfires doused in kerosene. There was no stopping a wagging tongue in the little Pebble Beach neighborhood. Folks had an inordinate amount of network connections and infinite time in which to be the catalyst for information. Both facts and fallacies were transported like a transcontinental bullet train.

"Jankovic family is seeking a tutor for their son."

By the time I personally got wind of the "talk," the son had jumped from nine to thirteen years old and was still in grade five. The previous tutor (me) got deported and the family was under investigation for harboring an illegal alien. If it wasn't sad, it would be comical. All the information was fabricated, which made my job of finding a replacement a formidable task.

Placed ads online and left notes with all the full-time teachers in Andrew's school. Several leads left me empty-handed until one senior woman stepped up and threw her off-the-chart fee on the table. Her interview went well, but I balked at the outrageous salary she demanded. Irina met the woman and agreed she fit the bill.

The plan, which *always* was altered, was that I would tutor one more week and leave right before Thanksgiving.

# Airline Ticket, Airline Ticket, Airline Ticket...

"Jill, we got your ticket back to Florida. You leave Monday at 7:30 a.m. from San Francisco."

Was I hearing correctly? "San Francisco is three hours from Pebble Beach, especially in traffic. If I have to be at the airport an hour before, that means I have to be there at 6:30. That also means we have to leave here at 3:00 in the morning. Are you serious?" I asked incredulously.

"You're right. I'll change it. Hang on." Irina pulled out her cell phone and made the trip work for an afternoon departure.

"Irina, what was the cost of the change?" My curiosity was piqued.

"It was two hundred dollars. But don't worry about it," she assured me nonchalantly.

"Wait, don't we have the other half of one of the flights you initially booked for me? Let's think this out."

"Don't worry. This will work." She paused. "Hold it. I should have made it from Monterrey. What was I thinking?" She tapped her forehead like a V-8 commercial.

"*Do not* change it again. I will leave on the flight you just booked." My frustration was growing, and it was not even my own money. Wastefulness goes against everything I believe in, and this was the epitome of being wasteful.

She spun away and returned less than ten minutes later. "You're leaving from Monterrey day after tomorrow. I hope that's OK, Jill."

"To where did you book it, girlfriend? What Florida city?"

She gasped. "Oh my God, I just assumed Miami would work. Is that near your house?"

"It doesn't matter." Florida is a long state, and there were several nearby airports. "It's fine." Mike would be picking me up, and he was not comfortable driving in the dark. We'd have to hire a car service but never mentioned it to Irina.

Mortgage payments and airline ticket changes travel in the same social circles.

# Boss Man Gets the News...

The cell phone rang the day before my scheduled departure. In a tone I'd not heard before—condescending, disapproving—Kep interrogated me like a criminal up for treason.

"Why are you leaving us so early? We have an agreement that you will tutor our son until the end of the year. It is a covenant, Jill." He was relentless. "I am tremendously disappointed."

It was six weeks Kep had been away on business. Forty-two days since we laughed over gin and tonics, discussed American politics, and debated religious creeds. We had parted friends, close friends, just a month and a half earlier, both assuming we'd see each other again. Another change in agenda left us bidding adieu over a telephone line.

His ranting continued and I had to interrupt him midstream.

"Stop it. Right now." My blood pressure was elevated. "You don't know the whole story, and it doesn't matter anyway."

"Jill." Silence for what seemed like eternity. "Are you leaving because the family is coming?" In seconds I realized my allegiances would be tested. I would never

188

betray Irina. I would also never betray Kep. The only way to eliminate any confrontation would be to fib.

"I'm leaving because my eye is acting up and I need to get back home to see my regular retina doctor."

"Is that the truth? Do you promise me that is the truth?" Kep drilled on. "Promise me, Jill. I'm waiting."

"Listen, Medicine Man, you're starting to annoy me. Sending a big hug to you." I finished my thought. "So sorry it's not in person. But our paths will cross again. I know it. The good Lord has plans."

"There *is* no good Lord. You know I'm an atheist."

"Kiss, kiss. May God be with you," I chided. Reluctantly ended the call, slipped my cell into my back pocket, and began to pack.

# And She's Off...

Sad good-byes carried me to my ride: the red pickup with giant lettering indicating a stud was piloting the muffler-less monster. As we slipped past the guard gate, an automatic reaction threw my face into my hands. Hated being seen perched up above the roadway in a vehicle that clearly did not belong in that zip code.

"Little lady, I'm gonna miss you." I turned slightly to offer a smile. "You were a lot of fun," he added. "A good sport."

"Thanks, Billy. I hope life works out the way you want. Can I offer some advice?" Reconsidered the discussion and decided to let it go. There would be too many suggestions relating to his persona, and at forty-four years old, he would not change anyway. "Never mind. Just enjoy life." I returned to my own thoughts.

One of the most rewarding experiences of my life was chauffeured to completion in a fire-engine-red, jacked-up truck piloted by a California character who believes the world was his playground.

Never envisioned this job would end with so little pomp and circumstance...

*Dear Diary,*

*Is that all there is?*

# Honey, I'm Home...

L eft the comfort and security of my Florida recliner to step on the other side of fear. Traversed the globe with the curiosity of a gal half my age fueled by dreams to make a difference in a child's life. Met a head of state, myriad millionaires, and a family who shrouded me with generosity. I became a faux relative blessed with benefits that made me a more informed person, more global, more adventuresome.

Secret dreams of Irina and Kep sit under lock and key in my heart. They have opened the portal to their souls to satisfy a fantasy not many senior citizens experience.

For the last four months it's been grandbaby visits, Taco Tuesdays with friends, and biking familiar paths throughout our gated community. We clip coupons and hit "early bird" dining specials the Sunshine State is famous for.

A transatlantic cruise is booked...to Ibiza. Called the family to see if they'd be around for a visit. They couldn't say where they'd be, but Bonita would be expecting us and opening up the main house for our use. Two weeks on the compound, visiting the British buds I met previously, grabbing meals at affordable, familiar haunts, some dancing on the Cala Pada shore. We'd stop to chat with Ursula at Hotel Arenal d'Or before hitting Aquas Blancas Beach.

*Dear Diary,*

*Do you know what makes stars twinkle? Magical keys, glazed in silver moonbeams. They fall from the heavens and hide between pages.*

# The Universe Has Its Own Agenda...

Five months after leaving California employment, a brief text flew across my cell: "Jill, we have a proposal for you. Call us."

*Dear Diary,*

*Feel like a pawn on the chessboard of life. When the queen makes her move, where will I be?*